The Philosophy of Mind

Studies in Philosophy

Consulting Editor:

V. C. Chappell

THE UNIVERSITY OF CHICAGO

THE
Philosophy
of Mind

Alan R. White

UNIVERSITY OF HULL, ENGLAND

RANDOM HOUSE | NEW YORK

Preface

With their usual generosity, my colleagues Mr. Roger
Montague, Mr. Richard Swinburne and Dr. Christopher
Williams, read through the whole of this book and re-
moved an enormous number of errors. My grateful thanks
are also due to Mr. Peter Geach and Prof. J. L. Mackie
for performing the same service. The many mistakes that
remain are due entirely to my own stubbornness and
stupidity.

The substance and much of the form of Chapter 3 appeared in my *Attention* (Blackwell, 1964). I have also
drawn on my lecture *Explaining Human Behaviour* (University of Hull Press, 1962) for part of Chapter 6. I am
indebted to the publishers of these works for permission to
re-use this material.

Contents

The Philosophy of Mind

CHAPTER 1

Introduction

The Meaning of "Philosophy"

The word "philosophy" is commonly used in two, not necessarily mutually exclusive, ways. In such phrases as "the Communist or American philosophy," "my philosophy of life," or "a liberal philosophy," it refers to a general set of attitudes and views, especially on moral, social and political matters. It is here synonymous with what in German is called *Weltanschauung*, or "outlook on life." An uneducated man who expresses an interest in questions of value, or who makes generalizations on life, such as "Women are all the same," is sometimes called "a bit of a philosopher." Perhaps because one of the earliest such philosophies—that preached by the Stoics—enjoined calmness and absence of emotion in time of trouble, we commend for his "philosophical" way of taking things someone who meets disaster with calm and balance.

The second common use of the word "philosophy" is to cover the type of inquiry pursued and the body of knowledge built up by those who in the past and the present are called "philosophers," in the same way that "history" and "chemistry" refer to the inquiries and findings that are associated with historians and chemists. Philosophy is a subject that may also be pursued and taught; it has its own history and its body of professionals. To find out what exactly philosophy is, as a subject, we would have to examine the writings of those who are generally called "philosophers."

Such an examination of the history of philosophy reveals, I think, that the subject has been something of a mixed bag, whose contents have been narrowed from the time of the Greeks—for whom philosophy (literally, "love of wisdom") covered every pursuit of knowledge—to contemporary analytic philosophers—for whom it is confined to conceptual analysis, that is, an examination of the logical features of the various concepts that we employ in our thinking. Historically, philosophers have studied sciences—such as mathematics, physics, biology, and psychology—evaluative systems and codes in morals, politics and aesthetics, and a heterogeneous group of subjects that includes theology, metaphysics, and logic. The contents of this mixed bag can, however, usefully be divided into three groups: (a) suggestions for a way of life, that is, a worked-out system of philosophy in what I called above the first use of "philosophy"; (b) contributions to the development of science; and (c) conceptual analysis. Sometimes groups (a) and (b) are combined as examples of first-order knowledge, concerned respectively with what ought to be and what is; group (c) is then contrasted with them, in a way to be explained shortly, as second-order knowledge of how we think about what ought to be and what is.

For reasons which we do not have space to go into now, I shall confine myself, as do most contemporary English-speaking philosophers, to group (c)—that is, to philosophy as the analysis of concepts and, particularly, of those concepts that we use in thinking about the mind and its functioning.

Conceptual Analysis

We can distinguish between an interest in understanding the world and an interest in understanding our understanding of the world. If we give the title of "first-order" to the questions and answers, investigations and theories, ideas and methods that are involved in attempting to understand or think about the world—whether it be animate or inanimate nature, the human or the divine, things scientific or things artistic, what is so or what ought to be so —then we can distinguish as "second-order" problems that have to do with these attempts to understand—that is, these questions and answers, investigations and theories, ideas and methods themselves. For instance, the question of what kinds of causes and motives make or lead people to commit certain kinds of crimes is a first-order problem, whereas the question of whether explanation in terms of motive excludes explanation in terms of cause, and also the questions of whether and, if so, why people of different ages and cultures seek for one or the other kind of explanation are second-order problems. The questions of how we are to attain knowledge of the constitution of the center of the earth, or of the prime numbers greater than a given prime, or of how to play the piano, are first-order problems; on the other hand, the questions of whether these are three different kinds of knowledge and whether children attain one kind earlier than the others are second-order problems. What sorts of things are valuable is a first-order question, while inquiries—whether psychological, sociological or logical—into our thinking about values are second-order.

An important distinction can be made, however, between different features of our understanding or thoughts of the world and, consequently, between different kinds of second-order questions. If our attention is devoted to discovering whether and why people at different historical times and in different cultures have employed different ways of trying to understand the world—e.g., whether they have employed both motive and causal explanations —then we are engaged in the sociology of knowledge. If, like the Swiss psychologist Piaget, we investigate how and at what stages children come to think about mathematical and empirical problems in the way that adults normally do, we are engaged in the psychology of knowledge. Both these attempts to understand our understanding are, for that very reason, second-order. Yet they are essentially of the same nature as our first-order attempts to understand the world, and employ the same scientific methods; they are part of psychology, sociology, anthropology, and history.

The feature of our understanding of the world that has interested philosophers from the earliest times is what we may call the "logical" relations among the various ideas, or ways of thinking, that we employ in our reflection upon and struggle with the problems of everyday life and of the arts and sciences. Practitioners of the various arts and sciences, as well as all of us in our everyday thinking, *employ* these ideas, or ways of thought; philosophers *examine* them. The latter wish to know, for example, how an explanation in terms of motives differs from an explanation in terms of causes; or how the knowledge we have of empirical matters, such as the core of the earth, differs from the knowledge we have of mathematical matters, such as the number of primes in a given range; or how knowledge of anything is related to belief about it and evidence for it. This distinction between philosophy as a second-order study and the sciences as, in general, first-order studies explains the traditional negative definition of philosophy as the subject that tackles those problems that are unanswerable by science.

In thinking about something in a particular way—that is, in using a particular idea, or concept, such as *motive, cause, knowledge, belief, mind* or *memory*—we take up a certain position with regard to what we are thinking about; we look at it in a certain way or put it into a particular category. To say that someone did not have a certain concept would be to say that he did not do this. In thinking of something in one way, we necessarily connect it with some of our other ways of thinking about things and disconnect it from still others, just as in taking up a physical position with regard to anything we erect a barrier against some parts of our surroundings while we leave a flank exposed to other parts, or in describing one point in space, we necessarily link it to, as well as separate it from, other points in space. For example, if we think, or say, that A *knows* that X is Y, we are logically committed to thinking, or saying, that X really is Y; on the other hand, if we think, or say, that A *believes* that X is Y, we are not thereby committed to thinking, or saying, that X really is Y. Thinking about something in a particular way—that is, using a particular concept—commits us in our further thinking to using certain other concepts about that same thing; to use the first concept is, partly or wholly, to use the second concept. What is *known* to be so is really so, whereas what is *believed* to be so need not be so. If I hold that X is totally included in Y and that Y is totally included in Z, then I am committed to holding that X is totally included in Z, because this is, under another guise or seen from another angle, at least part of what I held in the first place. A diagram of "X is totally included in Y and Y is totally included in Z," namely,

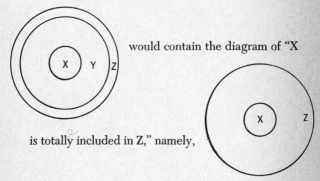

would contain the diagram of "X

is totally included in Z," namely,

When we take up a physical position, examination of this position shows us what other spatial positions it is near to or distant from, included in or excluded from, which positions it overlooks or is hidden from, which it is open to or blocked by, where it can most easily be attacked or defended. When we take up a position in thought, examination shows what other positions are contained in or excluded from our position, what supports it or rebuts it, what is relevant or irrelevant to it. Very much as physical

positions are spatially related, so positions in thought—
that is, concepts—are "logically" related. While physical
points include or exclude one another, the uses of concepts
imply or contradict one another. The philosopher's task is
to elucidate the network of inferences that one becomes
committed to by making a particular categorization of
things. He has to discover what the situations are in which
we can use a certain concept, what concepts precede or
follow it, of what set of concepts it is a part.

An examination of the logical features of the ways in
which we think about things—that is, of the concepts we
use—attempts to discover what is implied or excluded by
a given way of thinking, whether it supports or rebuts or
is merely irrelevant to something else we might think, and
whether to combine one way of thinking with another is
consistent or gives rise to contradictions. Further, we wish
to know how a given way of thinking is related to what it
is used to think about. Does it, for instance, describe it or
evaluate it, or endorse it; does it relate it to other things?
In discovering the relations of one way of thinking to other
ways—that is, the relation of the use of one concept to
that of other concepts—we are discovering the nature of
the concepts under examination. For concepts are, in this
respect, like mathematical points: they have no qualities
other than their relations to other concepts. Just as a
mathematical point has no size or any other quality, but
only its position relative to other points, which is indicated
by a set of co-ordinates, so a concept is defined by what
its use implies, contradicts, supports, rebuts, etc. Naming
a concept by mentioning the word that is used in a given
language to express it merely identifies the concept, just as
making a chalk mark on the blackboard merely provides
a representation of a mathematical point. Concepts are, of
course, in some respects unlike mathematical points. The
uses of concepts are related not only to each other but also
to the material in the world about which we use them.
We not only think in various ways, we also think about
various sorts of things. Further, whereas every point has
some other point standing to it in every possible spatial

relation, not every type of concept has every type of relation to one or another concept—for example, only relational concepts have converses.

Both the nature of a concept—that is, of a way of thinking—and a philosophical inquiry into it are best exemplified by considering briefly some of the ways in which we discover and test hypotheses about its logical features.

One way is to see what the use of the concept implies. The difference between thinking that something is beautiful and that it is colored is different in kind from the difference between thinking that something is colored and that it is old. For if A and B are identical in every other respect, then it follows that they are equal in beauty; but they could be identical in every other respect without being of the same color or of the same age.

A second way of discovering the logical features of a concept is to find out what questions may be appropriately asked about it. We can ask a man when he first realized that he had for years felt jealous of his sister and that she had felt jealous of him; but whereas we can ask him when he first realized that his sister had for years felt pains in her back, we cannot ask him when he first realized that he himself had for years felt pains in his back.

Similarly, we may look for the characteristics and qualifications that are relevant or irrelevant to the concept in question. If we *think about* a problem, we are doing something in which we may be engaged all morning, that we may be interrupted at, or may do to no avail; whereas, if we *think that* Hume was a greater philosopher than Locke, we are not doing something in which we can be engaged for a period, be interrupted at, or do with or without success. If a man believes that his wife has deceived him, his *belief* may be passionate and sincere enough, but too hasty and false; on the other hand, passion, sincerity, haste and falsity are not the sort of characteristics that we could either attribute to or deny of his friend's *knowledge* that the wife had been unfaithful.

Thirdly, we may put forward a hypothesis, or consider some hypothesis already put forward, about the logical

features of a certain concept and see whether it leads us
to contradictions, paradoxes or fantasies. For example,
some philosophers have held that the *meaning* of a phrase
is the object, or kind of object, to which the phrase refers,
as "motor car" refers to a kind of vehicle. If this theory
about the idea of *meaning* were true, then two phrases
that referred to the same object, or to the same kind of
object, would have the same meaning. But, although the
phrases "the Prime Minister of Great Britain during most
of the 1939–45 war" and "the famous descendant of Marl-
borough, known for his large cigars and his V-sign" both
refer to Winston Churchill, they obviously do not have the
same meaning. Further, one could understand either
phrase without knowing to whom it referred. Again, William James' theory that to say a belief is *true* is to say
that it works is refuted by the fact that we often find
that lies work, even in the long run, just as well as the
truth.

Fourthly, we may inquire how a concept is related to
whatever our thinking is about. This is to inquire what are
the kinds of situations and conditions in which it is used
or not used. For instance, if my wife asks me to transplant
the Masquerades, and I, not knowing much about roses,
dig up Peace, then I may plead I disturbed Peace *by
mistake;* whereas, if I trample on Peace in my attempts to
dig up the Masquerades, my plea is that I disturbed Peace
accidentally. If I am not certain about the concept of an
electron, I may ask whether tracks in cloud chambers are
related to scientists' assertions about electrons in the same
way as vapor trails in the sky are related to our assertions
about jet planes.

A philosophical examination of the concepts we use in
either our everyday or our specialized thinking consists,
therefore, in an attempt, by the methods mentioned, to
discover how the uses of these concepts are logically related to each other and to their subject matter. It consists
in revealing to us what is involved in the ways of thinking
that we employ. Nor is there anything strange about the
fact that a person may all his life employ quite correctly

certain concepts—and in this sense understand what he is doing—and yet be unable to say correctly how he does it and, therefore, be puzzled about these concepts. Most of us can speak grammatically, argue logically, or make and appreciate jokes, without knowing exactly how we do it. Augustine observed that he knew what time was, so long as he was not asked to say what it was. To say that some-one's views about a concept X are confused is not *per se* to deny that he uses the concept correctly. Philosophical analysts of ideas are related to the users of ideas somewhat as preachers are to practitioners, critics to poets, gram-marians to the native speakers of a language, map-makers to explorers, or Molière's philosopher to M. Jourdain, who had spoken prose all his life without realizing until then that it was prose.

Because we ordinarily think with the help of language, our ways of thinking are embodied in our ways of talking. To employ a concept is ordinarily to use a verbal expres-sion in a certain way; to indicate a concept is to mention a word or phrase. What we mean by a word "X," or by its synonyms "X_1" and "X_2," is our concept of X. Einstein's concept of relativity is what he meant by "relativity." If the word "X" has several meanings, it expresses several concepts. Hence, to discover the relations of one concept to another is to discover the relations of one meaning or use of a word both to other meanings or uses of the same word and to the meanings or uses of other words. An analysis of *interest* as an *inclination to pay attention* can take the linguistic form that to say that A is interested in Z is to say that he is inclined to pay attention to Z. Two people could use the same word differently, but they could not use the same concept differently; for the so-called "difference in the use of a concept" is really the use of a different concept, just as a difference in the spatial co-ordinates of a point makes it a different point. What con-cept a man is employing depends not on what word he uses, but on how he uses the word. If A and B use the same word differently, then they are not expressing the same concept by it. Furthermore, once we have plotted some of the relations of a given concept, as of a given point, to others, then other relations necessarily follow from that.

The Nature of the Philosophy of Mind

Among the many concepts and, therefore, linguistic expressions, of daily life and of the works of novelists and historians, are those in which we think, or talk, about the mental qualities and powers, traits and abilities, character and behavior, feelings and experiences, of ourselves and of others. For instance, we are employing various species of the concept of *intelligence* when we use such familiar adjectives as "clever," "silly," "logical," "imprudent," and "skillful." The concept of *will* is involved in our descriptions of acts as "voluntary," "involuntary," "responsible," or "my own fault." The ideas expressed by "interest," "enjoyment," "consciousness," "care," "negligence," and "concentration" all have to do with the concept of *attention*. Our explanations of human behavior involve the use of "motive," "intention," "purpose," "inclination," and "desire." A huge range of human experience is understood in terms of various concepts of *feeling*; we may "feel" headaches or half-crowns, we may "feel" hot, depressed, optimistic, or indignant, we may "feel" like writing to the papers or "feel" that we have been a failure.

The examination of such mental concepts is of use not only to the philosopher, but also to those whose chief interest is in the science of psychology. For many of the concepts of such a science have either been taken over bodily from daily use or else have been shaped and sharpened into tools of science from their original place in our ordinary language. Even when a quite new concept is introduced into psychology, it must be related to and explainable in terms of the concepts we understand in our common everyday judgments about people; otherwise we could not see the relevance of psychology to such everyday judgments. Despite the denials of some psychologists, what they label as "habits," "traits," and "attitudes" bear very close resemblances to what we ordinarily call by such names. We would not allow them to decide the educational future of our children unless we thought that their "intelligence tests" measured something very like what we normally think of as intelligence and its manifestations. The technical concept of *motivation* covers our ordinary concept of *motive*, even though it is also, perhaps confusedly, stretched to cover almost every sort of explanation of human behavior.

The examination of our everyday and our technical mental concepts is the philosophy of mind. It has two important negative characteristics.

(a) The first is that such an examination does not attempt to dispute or add to any facts about the mind that are accepted by the scientist or the ordinary man. One should not expect from it any new information of an empirical kind, nor should one reproach it for not using the experimental and observational methods of the practicing psychologist. To accuse the philosopher of mind of armchair-psychology is as misleading as to claim for him any special insight. "It shows," said Wittgenstein, "a fundamental misunderstanding, if I am inclined to study the headache I have now in order to get clear about the philosophical problem of sensation."

For several reasons, this negative characteristic of philosophical inquiry needs to be especially stressed in connection with psychology. In the first place, many of the great philosophers of the past, such as Plato, Aristotle, and the British Empiricists, Locke, Berkeley, and Hume, inextricably mixed psychological with philosophical inquiries into the human mind, so that their writings are rightly quoted in histories of either of these subjects. Nor has this assimilation of the two inquiries altogether ceased to be made today; philosophers are still fond of what they call "Phenomenology." Thus, in direct contrast to the comment just quoted from Wittgenstein are the following two pronouncements, the first from the seventeenth-century philosopher Locke and the second from G. E. Moore in the twentieth century. Locke began his investigation of *perception* with the statement, "What perception is, everyone will know better by reflecting on what he does himself, when he sees, hears, feels, etc., or thinks, than by any discourse of mine. Whoever reflects on what passes in his own mind cannot miss it. And if he does not reflect, all the words in the world cannot make him have any notion of it." Moore said that his aim was "to analyse the mental occurrence—the act of consciousness—which we call seeing" and that "all of us who are not blind can directly observe the mental occurrence, which we mean by seeing."

Secondly, it is easy to suppose that philosophy has a closer connection with psychology than with any other inquiry because there is, as we saw in the previous section, a sense in which part of psychology is, like philosophy, a second-order study. In the psychology of thought, we study our thinking rather than the world we think about. It is significant in this connection that the chief philosophical works of Locke and Hume were entitled respectively *An Essay Concerning Human Understanding* and *A Treatise of Human Nature*. Psychology, unlike physics or chemistry, cannot be distinguished from philosophy simply in terms of the material it studies, since there are psychological as well as philosophical examinations of concepts. Some philosophers today would consider the work of the psychologist Piaget on the acquisition and growth of logical, mathematical, and moral concepts among children to be of more philosophical relevance than, say, the work of Einstein or of Darwin.

But though both philosophy and one sector of psychology examine our thinking, our use of concepts, rather than the material upon which this thinking operates, their interests in it are entirely different. Empirical questions about the origin, acquisition, and deployment of our concepts, about the connections between them and our abilities and emotions, and about the intellectual capacities of children and adults, of the stupid and the brilliant, the normal and the pathological, are quite different from conceptual questions about the logical relations between various kinds of concepts, such as *thought, imagination, perception,* and *memory.* It was simply a mistake on the part of the empiricist philosophers in the eighteenth century not to distinguish psychological and genetic questions about the acquisition of ideas from conceptual questions about the logical criteria of claims to knowledge.

(b) The second negative characteristic of a philosophy of mind is that it makes no attempt to dispute, change, or justify the concepts that we employ in thinking about the human mind and human behavior, and which we all use and follow without difficulty in our adult thinking. Changes of that kind are the business of those who use the concepts, not of those who examine this use. The philosopher's task is to inquire into the logical features possessed by these concepts, not to suggest that we should use other concepts. This is not to say, however, that he may not *en route* dispute other philosophers' analyses and the views of reflective men about such concepts. The touchstone of a philosophical theory about the mind—that is, a theory about mental concepts—is its faithfulness to the actual use of these concepts.

The Importance of the Philosophy of Mind

In the previous section, I referred to the distinction between using a concept and describing, or giving an account of, that use. The former is something that most of us can do quite well with the concepts of our daily thinking; we ordinarily have no difficulty in using, or understanding others in their use of, such concepts as *motive, inclination, attention, care, habit, intelligence, will,* and *feeling.* Similarly, the professional psychologist is usually quite at home with the technical conceptual tools of his trade and easily follows the shop talk of his colleagues. But expertness in the use of conceptual tools, whether ordinary or technical, is not incompatible with confusion in an exposition of their use. Plato and Aristotle, Locke and Hume, Descartes and Ryle, probably had no superiority over one another, or over us, in their use and understanding of the manifold mental concepts; but they have given different and mutually incompatible interpretations of the nature of these concepts. The question which, if any, interpretation is correct is surely as important as a number of other celebrated questions in man's pursuit of knowledge.

Quite apart from its intrinsic worth, however, an attempt to understand the concept of *mind* and other mental concepts is useful for those who, whether they are psychologists or laymen, are interested in trying to understand the mind itself. In psychology, perhaps more than in most other sciences, the way to progress in empirical investigations is sometimes barred by conceptual confusion. Several causes may be suggested for this conceptual confusion.

First, in dealing with what may be called "mental characteristics" we are working in a less tangible and more inaccessible field than are those who work in the natural sciences; it is a field in which theories are less easily tested, where the use of instruments and observation seems to be more difficult, and where the subject-matter of our study seems less easy to locate and to hold. Hence, our talk and our thought about our subject-matter seems less precise, less anchored to what is publicly inspectable. Secondly, perhaps because of what we have just mentioned, most of the concepts we use in reference to the mind are expressed in metaphorical and analogical language, which it is always tempting to take literally or unanalogically. We speak of "deep" or "shallow," "quick" or "slow," minds; we "focus" our attention or "summon up" our interest; we "search" for an idea and perhaps fail to "grasp" it; we "store" information in our head or "at the back of" our mind; we "acquire" and "lose" opinions; we "burn" with desire or are "pricked" by our conscience; we are "torn" with anxiety and are "full" of confidence. If we do not take these phrases literally, then how are we to take them? We shall see how entire theories of mind, as well as particular views on individual mental concepts, arise from pressing these analogies in one direction or another.

Thirdly, there are various natural assumptions we are inclined to make when we think about the mind, because analogous moves are quite legitimate in other fields. We assume, for instance, that to talk about the mind is to talk of an entity—albeit a mysterious entity—called "mind," because to talk about the body is to talk of an entity called "body"; and that just as "body" is the name of something that I have, so "I" or "the Ego" is the name of something—e.g. a mind—that has it. We assume that, since knowledge can be acquired, it must, like our material possessions, be located somewhere, whence it can be produced on demand. We assume that, since many verbs refer to things that people do—such as to walk, to talk, to run, or to jump—then "to know" and "to believe" refer to something, perhaps something mental, that people do. We assume that, since "counting" and "digging" each refers to one particular type of activity in which we may engage, so also "thinking" and "paying attention" each refers to one particular activity in which we may engage. What enables these natural assumptions to retain their hold on us is that when we fail to discover, for example, the entity called "mind," the place where we "store" our knowledge, the act we perform when "knowing," or the particular activity signified by "paying attention," then, instead of surrendering the assumption, we readily accept the explanation that these alleged entities, places, acts, or activities are "mental," "immaterial," "non-substantial," "abstract," or "mysterious."

A fourth cause of conceptual confusion in amateur and technical views about mental characteristics arises from the deserved popularity of problems about man's mind and human behavior. Speculation about the mind is a natural thing; it is something that few intelligent and educated people do not indulge in at some time or another. Naturally also it has been, since the dawn of philosophical thought, a favorite field for speculation; there is probably no major philosopher who has not advanced some views on this topic. No educated man today can begin to reflect upon mental concepts without being from the outset burdened in his reflections by the heritage of his culture, by the views of Greek philosophers or Christian theologians, and of moral, political, social, and scientific writers of all ages.

Fifthly—and perhaps most important—in psychology, far more than in any other science, the establishment of theories has, at least until very recently, largely relied on and sprung from considerations and evidence of a conceptual rather than of an observational or experimental kind. By this I mean that when, for example, Plato and many later psychologists divided the mind into three parts, their reasons, as we shall see, were often such conceptual considerations as the fact that we speak of *wishing* to do so and so, but *restraining* ourselves because we *realize* it would be wrong to do it. When a recent introductory book on memory calls remembering an "activity" and retaining a "process," and declares that forgetting is a "process not directly observable in itself, which produces a decrement in remembering"; or when St. Augustine speaks of memory as "an inner place which is yet no place," the evidence for these suggestions has not been gathered from observation or experiment, but from assumptions about the use of concepts. To examine the experimental basis of a scientific theory is a matter for scientists; to examine its conceptual foundations, however, is to philosophize.

Although a person may handle his concepts with complete competence, and even use them fruitfully in his amateur or professional inquiries into human nature, without being able to give an explicit and correct account of the nature of these concepts, there is an important point at which misapprehensions about them can hinder and vitiate his inquiries. In tackling any problem we have to make assumptions, either explicit or implicit, about the nature of our problem, and, hence, about the appropriate ways in which to tackle it. For instance, we use our eyes and optical instruments in a piece of research because we assume that what we are in search of is visible. If it is only audible, then our methods of inquiry are doomed to failure. The failure in the seventeenth and eighteenth centuries to arrive at an understanding of combustion, and the consequent introduction of an element with negative weight, called "phlogiston," was due to the assumption that, in the process of burning, something is emitted from a metal. It was the assumptions of classical mechanics as to the absolute character of times and lengths that led to the impasse in physics from which it was freed by Einstein's theory of relativity. Psychology has suffered in the same way. "It is astonishing," said William James, "what havoc is wrought in psychology by admitting at the outset apparently innocent suppositions, that nevertheless contain a flaw." We get strange answers, in short, because we ask the wrong questions.

Let me mention here two examples of such false assumptions, which I shall discuss in detail in Chapters 4 and 5. The first concerns the concept of *thought*. For centuries psychologists tried to discover the nature of thought by watching themselves as they did some thinking. Because what they often observed in such cases was a series of images, some were led to suppose that thinking consisted in the having or manipulating of images. Later experiments by the Wurzburg School showed, however, that in many cases subjects went through long trains of thought without using any images. What was not realized, except in part by later members of the school, was that the basic assumption underlying the experiments was mistaken. It is not the presence of images or words or any other material that constitutes thinking; it is the fact that this, or any other material, is being used for a particular purpose, such as to solve a problem. The mistaken assumption was that to describe someone as "thinking" is to describe a specific, perhaps mental, activity in which he is engaged, in the same way as is true when we describe him as "talking," "humming," "muttering," or "having images." This is, however, a conceptual mistake of exactly the same kind as the assumption that "repetition" is the name of a specific kind of activity in which we may be engaged, alternatively to talking or humming. There is no specific activity called "repeating"; it is merely the doing of anything whatsoever for the second or *n*th time.

The second example of experimentation based on a false

conceptual assumption comes from investigations into the nature of *emotion*, such as fear, love, pity, or indignation. The philosophers Descartes and Hume in the seventeenth and eighteenth centuries and the psychologists Wundt and Titchener in the nineteenth century tried to discover what fear and indignation were, by introspective methods that were designed to isolate the phenomenon of fear or of indignation. In a similar way, some twentieth-century psychologists tried to isolate the physiological changes that are thought to occur when we become afraid, in the belief that by so doing they would discover the nature of fear. All these experiments, from Descartes on, however valuable in themselves, failed to discover the nature of fear, because they all went on the assumption that the concept of *emotion* is like the concept of *image* or the concept of *bodily change*—that is, that it indicates some isolable occurrence in us. But it is part of the concept of *emotion* that emotions are directed to something. A fear of the dentist is different from a fear that one's political opponents will win the next election, and also from the fear of falling off a chair, precisely because these fears have different objects. Even though the object of one's fear may not actually exist, "fear" is not the name of some isolable phenomenon, either mental or physiological, whose nature is independent of the nature of its object. Further, what makes us call something "fear" rather than, say, "awe" is not any observed introspective or physiological difference, but the fact that the object feared is one we also wish to avoid. Similarly, what makes a feeling one of "indignation" rather than of "anger" is not an unobserved introspectable or physiological phenomenon, but the fact that the object of our feelings is thought to be in some way unfair. One can be angry with oneself, but not indignant with oneself.

Finally, it is not only insofar as they may become the source of irrelevant empirical investigations and experiments that conceptual errors are important, but also as the cause of many of our beliefs, in areas where investigation and experiment play little part. Theological beliefs, for instance, sometimes rest on conceptual rather than empirical evidence. A belief in fatalism often derives from confusion between the ideas of logical necessity and of physical inevitability. One of my aims in this book will be to show that much of what is commonly believed about the mind and its place in nature is based on our assumptions about the logical relations among our mental concepts.

Apart from its intrinsic interest, therefore, the importance of the philosophy of mind is that it clears up or helps to avoid the conceptual confusion that blocks progress in the useful employment of our correct empirical data, that leads to a waste of effort and to illogical hypotheses, and that is one source of our mistaken beliefs on many matters of moment.

CHAPTER 2

Theories of the Mind

Before examining individual mental concepts, such as *attention, interest, consciousness, thought, feeling, motive,* and *intention,* it is worth sketching some of the general pictures of the mind that have prevailed in European thought from Plato to the present day, in order to show the extent to which they are based on assumptions as to what is implied in our everyday thought and talk about the mind.

As a preliminary, let us note two points of logic. First, we can say both that a body has a head, a torso, and four limbs, and that it has food in it and clothes on it. Whereas the body is distinct from its food and its clothes, however, it *is* its head, torso, and four limbs organized in certain ways. When we have seen these elements, we have seen the body. The body is not an object over and above its parts, in the way that it is an object over and above its food and its clothes. One question we have to ask about the mind is whether it is related to our mental abilities and dispositions, our thoughts and feelings, as the body is related to its limbs or as the body is related to its food. Philosophers who speak of the mind as the container of our thoughts and the owner of our feelings look on the mind in the latter way. Secondly, although the body is not an object additional to its parts, the organization of the parts of the body does constitute an organized object, namely, the body—of the same kind as any one of the parts. We can ask the same sorts of questions about the body as we can about its parts, particularly questions about its location. I shall say that a word names an entity, if it names something that is related, either as the body is to its food or as the body is to its legs. Now, contrast with the concept of *body* the concept of *British Constitution*. "British Constitution" signifies the ways in which the Church, the Sovereign, the Judicature, the Parliament, and the laws of Britain are organized relative to each other. It is neither the name of an element added on to these others, nor is it the name of an organized object that is composed of them. In short, it does not name an entity.

Our historical sketch will show that most philosophers and psychologists—with the partial exception of Aristotle —have until quite recently commonly assumed that the word "mind" ("soul," "spirit," etc.) is used as the name of an entity in the same way as, for example, "body" is the name of an entity. That is, they have assumed that the mind is something of which it makes sense to ask such questions as "Where is it?," "Of how many, if any, parts is it composed?," "How is it related to other entities, especially the body?" As an entity, mind is said to have a place of existence (although it may not occupy space), to enter into causal relations with other entities, and to be distinguishable and observable in itself and not merely through its manifestations. It is said to contain our thoughts. It is upon this common assumption that several quite different theories of the mind have been based.

The Political Theory

In his book on the constitution of an ideal state, the *Republic*, Plato proposed a theory of the mind (or psyche) that was expressly modeled on a political community. The human mind is regarded as a microcosm of human politics, and mental concepts are interpreted in political language. Nor is this analogy—whose persuasiveness no doubt sprang from the well-developed political language and thought that Greek thinkers of the fifth and fourth centuries B.C. inherited as part of their culture—of merely antiquarian interest. The metaphors of our ordinary descriptions of human conduct and the concepts of our moral thinking are still largely colored by these political and legal analogies. We compare our deliberations and decisions with those of political assemblies, we discuss our indecisions and conflicts and our worries about right and wrong in terms of legal disputes. We listen to or reject the "authority of conscience" and we bring our cases "before the bar of reason." Our self-control is likened to the control of law and government over rebels and rioters—who, in this case, are our greed, our lust, and our terror. The moral system of Butler, in which conscience holds legal authority over our various principles and passions, and that of Kant, in which we are all part of a moral kingdom where each of us is both sovereign and subject, owe much to this constitutional analogy. As a matter of history, most Western views about the mind up to at least the sixteenth century —whether in philosophy, theology, or general literature— were only variations on the schemes of Plato and Aristotle.

Plato supposed, in his *Phaedo*, that "mind" (or "psyche") is the name of an invisible entity which, in conjunction with or separate from the body, is capable of acquiring knowledge. The conceptual and analogical nature of his approach to a theory of mind comes out clearly in two of his attempts to prove that the mind is something that has existed before it enters into and gives life to our body.

First, he insists (*Phaedo* 70c–72b) that "It is necessary that everything that has an opposite comes to be from its opposite"—that is, that if A becomes X, it must have become X from being not-X. For instance, what becomes smaller (weaker, worse, or just) becomes so from being bigger (stronger, better, or unjust), and *vice versa*. Hence, since "living" and "dead" are the names of opposites, the living must have become living from being dead. So far Plato's argument is impeccable, for it is a logical truth that, if A becomes X, it must have been other than X before. But this does not prove what Plato wants—namely, that what is alive must have come from what is dead, and that there must be something in the land of the dead from which things in the land of the living can come. He thinks that he has proved this only because he confuses a logical principle—that what becomes X could only have become so from having previously been the opposite of X—with a similar-sounding but causal principle that what becomes X *must have come from*—that is, must have been produced out of—the opposite of X. To say that A becomes X from being not-X is not to say, as Plato does, that A becomes X from not-X. If I become rich, I must, to be sure, have previously been poor; but my riches did not "come from" my poverty. Becoming rich from being poor is not like becoming rich from being thrifty. To say that what becomes alive becomes so from being dead is not to say that what becomes alive becomes so from the dead. To acquire life from being dead—that is, after having previously been dead—is not to acquire life from death. Similarly, the logical truth that what comes into existence must previously not have existed does not contradict the old causal law that nothing can come from what does not exist (*ex nihilo nihil fit*). Plato has given no good reason to suppose, therefore, that there must be a land of the dead from which life (or the soul) comes into our bodies.

In his second proof (*Phaedo* 73c–76e), Plato tries to show that much of our knowledge must be a recollection of something learned before we were born—that is, by our pre-existing mind. One of his reasons for this view arises as follows. It is a common experience to observe that something which is Xish may not be absolutely or entirely X. For instance, however equal two sticks may be, they may not be absolutely equal; however beautiful or good or just—or, we may add, however large or round or happy—anything may be, it is not absolutely beautiful or good, etc. If, says Plato, an Xish thing is not absolutely X, we can say that it is like X, but "falls short of" being X or is "unable to be" X. Then, he holds, it follows that "Whoever thinks this must of necessity have previous knowledge of the thing which he says the other resembles but falls short of." Since nothing in the world, he believes, is absolutely equal or beautiful or just, our knowledge of the absolutely equal or beautiful or just, which these things fall short of, must have been acquired by our minds before they came into our bodies. Therefore, our minds must have existed previously.

The philosophically important thing to notice here is the conceptual assumption on which Plato's argument rests—namely, that to recognize that A is not quite or absolutely or entirely X implies that we know or have an idea of what it is for something to be absolutely or entirely X, and that it is by comparing A to this that we see that it falls short. That this is a very plausible assumption is clear from the fact that it occurs in later thinkers and in other contexts. It is the assumption made in one of Descartes' arguments in the third *Meditation* for the existence of God, and it is shared as well by some theological writers. "How could I know," says Descartes, "that something is wanting to me and that I am not wholly perfect, if I possessed no idea of a being more perfect than myself, by comparison with which I knew the deficiencies of my nature?" The same assumption underlies a commonly accepted theory about thought—namely that, when we are looking for the right word for an idea that we have, what enables us to reject various suggestions as inadequate and accept one as being right is that during our search we have before our mind the thought we are trying to express and that it is against this that the alternatives are sized up.

What gives this assumption its plausibility is that in many cases we do in fact say that A is "not X" or "not absolutely X" on the strength of our knowing what X is, to the extent of having a sample or an idea of X with which we compare A. For instance, we compare the liquid in the not quite full glass with the whole glass; we compare the alleged indigo-blue with the color chart; we accept a pattern because it fits the template and we reject a glove because it does not fit the hand. It is, however, a conceptual mistake to suppose that recognition of imperfection in A implies a knowledge of what perfection would be. Nor is that always true in fact. A candidate's examination paper is given less than top grade, not necessarily because the examiner has a specimen of the perfect paper, but because he can see how the candidate's paper might have been better. If I can see how A might be rounder or more beautiful, how B might be more charitable or more just, or how A and B might be more equal than they are, then that enables me to see that A is not absolutely round or big or beautiful, that B does not show perfect charity or justice, and that A and B are not exactly equal. I do not have to know what absolute circularity or beauty or charity or justice or equality is. More importantly, I could not see that, for example, a particular number is not quite as great as it might be by comparing it with the greatest number, for there neither is nor could there be a greatest number with which to compare the given number. I do not *have to* know, and sometimes *cannot* know, the perfect in order to recognize the existence of imperfections.

Let us now look at the details of the picture that Plato gave of the constitution of this alleged entity, the mind. As I have said, he models it on a political community. Believing, for reasons we need not discuss, that a community can be divided into three elements—roughly describable as the governing element, the executive element, and the productive element—he suggested that the human mind could be divided into three analogous and analogously related elements. These he called the rational element, the spirited element, and the element of desire. Just as, in a state, the governing element relies on the executive element to support it and enforce its directives to the producers for the wellbeing of the community, so in a wellbalanced mind reason is aided by determination in its attempts to direct, encourage, and restrain a man's desires. In the *Phaedrus* (245c–257), the three elements of the mind are pictured as a charioteer (the rational element) driving an obedient horse (the spirited element) and a disobedient horse (the element of desire), although in a passage in the

Phaedo (94b), the mind is thought of as being wholly rational and regulative, the other elements being attributed to the body.

The picture of the mind as something that is divisible into three parts has been very common. The triad of cognitive, affective, and conative—which some historians of psychology trace back to Kant's faculties of knowing, feeling, and willing, but which is utimately a variation on Plato's scheme—has colored most of the psychology of the last century. Nor, as we shall see, is it unconnected with the Freudian trinity of Ego, Super-ego, and Id. Indeed, in a famous passage in the *Republic* (571), Plato anticipates Freud's view of dreaming as the occasion on which our less respectable desires break out, while the governing element of the mind is asleep. (Freud also uses Plato's analogy of the charioteer.) Aristotle, too, has a triple division of the powers of the mind. For the moment, however, let us concentrate on Plato's theory, in order to bring out how his reasons for this tripartite political view of the mind depend on analogies and on assumptions about the use of concepts.

One of his arguments is that, if a community has certain characteristics, then by analogy the members of that community must have these characteristics. An alleged proof of this is that the cause of national characteristics lies in personal characteristics, as when we explain the excitability of the French nation, the stolidity of the Germans, or the fecklessness of the Irish by these characteristics in the individual citizens of these countries. It does not, however, follow from this that, inasmuch as a community is composed of three elements, each of its members is therefore composed of three elements, much less that personal tripartitism is the cause of national tripartitism. The fecklessness of the Irish nation is the fecklessness of individual Irishmen, but the partition of Ireland arises not from a partition within individual men, but from the partition between them.

A second alleged proof that what holds for the community holds for the individual is based on the principle that "if to two things we give the same name, then they are in that respect alike." Since to call the state "just" is, according to Plato, to say that each of its three elements does its own work, to call a citizen of the state "just" is similarly to assert that each element of his mind does its proper work. But the principle appealed to here is vague; it does not work in the same way for all concepts. What allows us to call a man "thirty years old," "Western," or "tripartite" is exactly what allows us to call a state "thirty years old," "Western," or "tripartite"; but what allows us to call a man "large" or "rich"—namely, that his bulk or wealth is more than that of most men—does not allow us to call a state "large" or "rich." What allows us to call a state "good" or "free" is not necessarily any more like what allows us to call a man "good" or "free" than it is like what allows us to call a wheel "good" or "free." The concept of *justice*, to which Plato applied his principle, is more like those of *richness, freedom,* and *goodness* than it is like those of *thirty, Western,* and *tripartite.* Even if it were true that a just state is one in which all the classes minded their own business, that is not the hall-mark of a just decision, a just law, or a just man.

Plato's second main argument for a tripartite division of the mind is based on further conceptual assumptions. Faced with the fact that there are different sorts of things we do, he asks, "Do we learn with one part of ourselves, feel anger with another and with a third desire the pleasures of nutrition and generation and their kind, or is it with the entire soul that we function in each case?" Note the way in which he sets about answering this question. "It is obvious," he says, "that the same thing will never do or suffer opposites in the same respect in relation to the same thing and at the same time." For example, if a man is standing in the one place, but moving his hands and his head, we should not say, insists Plato, that the man is both moving and at rest, but that one part is at rest and the other in motion. Since to desire something and to refrain from it are opposites, they cannot be done at the same time by the same thing. When, therefore, someone wants to drink and yet—perhaps because he knows it is wrong, or because someone else needs the drink more—he restrains himself, we must, in Plato's opinion, say that there is one thing (the element of desire) in the mind that bids him drink and another thing (the reason) that forbids him. When a man's desires get the better of his determination, we must suppose that one element temporarily defeats another element. To say of children that they are always wanting things and are full of high spirits, but have not yet reached the age of discretion, is to say, according to this theory, that their desiring and spirited elements are more developed than their rational element. A corollary of Plato's assumption about opposites, which philosophers have sometimes not hesitated to draw, is that each of the three supposed divisions of the mind would have to be further subdivided into myriad other parts. Since a man may not only find himself, as we say, drawn one way by desire and another way by reason, but may also be a prey to conflicting desires and remain undecided between different rational alternatives, are we to have a sub-element for each different desire and a sub-element for each different logical alternative?

There is, however, no necessary reason for accepting Plato's assumptions about opposites or about the nature of desire. First of all, what restrains a man from indulging every momentary desire need not be an opposite element called "reason." It may be a habit, perhaps laboriously acquired, of not doing anything without considering its consequences; similarly, what prevents him from doing what he thinks he should do may be nothing more than an indolent disposition. In the same way, "determination" signifies the ability to persist or resist, and "conscientiousness" signifies a habit of not skimping anything. But abilities and habits, as we shall see, are not entities or elements. To explain a man's fortitude or his scrupulousness, his weakness or his lack of conscience, in the face of temptation is not at all to show him as made up of opposing elements, but as one man who by nature or training meets, or fails to meet, certain kinds of situations in certain sorts of ways. Secondly, although ordinarily the man who proposes the rules is different both from the man who sees that they are carried out and from the man who wishes to circumvent them, there is no reason why the same man should not be inclined both to submit to and to avoid rules that he himself set up, to apply as much to himself as to others. Thirdly, desiring to do X and desiring not to do X are not opposites, like moving toward X and retreating from X.

Such is the conceptual, non-empirical, nature of the reasons advanced by Plato for his picture of the mind as an entity with a composition analogous to that of a political community.

The Physical Theory

The grand assumption that underlies Plato's picture of the mind, as well as some of the religious views of the soul during the Middle Ages, was that where our language suggests that we are naming an entity, and yet we can find no physical body, there is instead a spirit. This assumption was still prevalent at the time of the rise of modern science. Nor was it confined merely to the concept of *mind*. In a similar way, other mental concepts—such as *thought, idea, emotion, desire, knowledge,* and *intelligence*—were assumed to refer to particular non-physical entities or processes, each of which had a location "in the mind."

In 1649 Descartes said, "All that is in us, and that we cannot anywise view as appertaining to a body, has to be attributed to the soul." But that of which Descartes thought that "mind" (or "soul") was the name was not viewed by him, as it was by Plato, on analogy with a political body, but on analogy with the physical processes, which the energetic science of mechanics was beginning to describe with such success.

One fact that made this physical analogy persuasive was that the ordinary terms for describing the things of the mind are largely borrowed from the language in which we describe physical phenomena. Minds can be deep or dirty, slow or tenacious, dull or flashing; they can be "weighed down" by worry or "lightened" by good news. We can "bear" something in mind or "cast it out." We can be "numbed" by desire or by an electric shock, "torn" between patriotism and ambition or between two physical forces. We can be "aroused" by jealousy or by a loud noise. We can "display" courage or a light; we can "possess" plenty of ambition and little knowledge, or much property and little cash. Either our feet or our feelings can be "hurt." Just as Plato was persuaded to take semi-literally those metaphorical descriptions of our self-control and our determination, our deliberations and our decisions, that are borrowed from the rich language of political theory, so the contemporaries and successors of Descartes gave a semi-literal interpretation to the physical language in which we express many of our thoughts about the mind.

A second factor that favored a physical analogy for the mind was the great advances in the natural sciences in the sixteenth and seventeenth centuries, which led men to believe that other areas of inquiry should be examined in a parallel way. Yet the power of their religious thought, with its respect for the immortal soul, prevented them from completely assimilating the mental to the physical. Mechanics studied machines. Animals, Descartes held, were only complicated unfeeling machines; yet it would be sacrilege to think that man was nothing more than a machine. Physical words stand for physical elements, and mental words must stand in an analogous way for analogous mental elements. Man must be a body plus a mind.

Hence, from the seventeenth century onwards, the current theories of the mind have been modeled on physics, later on chemistry and physiology and, more recently, on cybernetics. An analogy is drawn between physics and psychology, between the physical world and the mental, between body and mind, between physical or chemical elements and mental elements, between physical gravitation and mental association, between the vibrations of matter and the sensations of mind. Just as Galileo tried to discover the basic elements from which the furniture of the world is built, the alphabet in which the Book of Nature is written, so Locke sought the simple ideas with which the cabinet of the mind is furnished. For Descartes, the body is an "extended thing" and the mind a "thinking thing," the latter being lodged in the former. For Locke, who was a contemporary of Newton, the mind was an "empty cabinet" gradually furnished with ideas acquired during our life, a "sheet of white paper painted upon" by experience. Later in the eighteenth century Hume, on one occasion, likened the mind to "a kind of theater, where several perceptions successively make their appearance; pass, repass, glide away, and mingle in an infinite variety of postures and situations." He modeled his views about the association of ideas upon Newton's laws of gravitation: "a kind of attraction, which in the mental world will be found to have as extraordinary effects as in the natural." Newton's theories similarly provided a model for Hartley. In the nineteenth century the "mechanical association" of James Mill was replaced by the "mental chemistry" of his son John Stuart Mill. The acquisition of ideas and knowledge was likened to the construction of a chemical compound from simple elements. The psycho-physics of Fechner and early work in Factor Analysis seemed to some to bring the support of physiology to this general picture of the mind.

Sometimes this analogy between physical and mental concepts, and also between the objects to which they allegedly referred, was taken negatively. The mental was everything that the bodily was not. Just as physical objects were out in the open—public and perceivable by all with healthy sense organs—and related to each other in various ways that were explicable in the causal terms of mechanics, so the supposed mental objects were immaterial, did not exist in space, were not open to public view by any of the five senses, and could not be accounted for by any of the causal laws of physics. Quickly, however, these negative descriptions gave way to positive assertions. The mind and its contents existed, it was held, as mental or spiritual "things." They were inside us, perhaps in the head. Each person had a special private access to the contents of his own mind, and this access was by a special method of perception called "introspection." Motives, purposes, and desires were regarded as physical causes operating on psychical entities.

Whether a negative or a positive view was taken of the mind and its characteristics, it was natural to ask how this supposed entity, the mind, and its contents were related to the body and its qualities. Is there an inexplicable but pre-ordained independent parallelism between the physical elements and the psychical? Or do they interact, so that physical events are able to affect psychical states, and *vice versa*? Or are mental contents related in some other way to physical elements?

Various consequences followed from this picture of the mind. If one said that "desire numbed me" or that "anger drove him," these were interpreted as meaning that a mental entity had an effect on a physical entity in a way analogous to that in which one physical object might affect another. Conversely, it was thought that a man's jealousy might be aroused by a word in somewhat the way the man himself might be aroused by a knocking at the door. The behavior of a man, as contrasted with that of a machine, or even of an animal, was thought of as the outward and visible effects of an inward and invisible change in the constitution of his mind. The direct knowledge that our senses give us of our bodies is paralleled by that which they give us of other people's bodies; but there is, at least outside telepathy, no direct knowledge of another's mind comparable to the direct knowledge that introspection gives us of our own.

When we submit this picture of the mind to philosophical scrutiny, it is not our job to support or deny any of the facts that it attempts to explain, but only to criticize the explanation it gives of them. Nor do we criticize this explanation for any faults it may have of an observational or experimental nature. What interests us is the conceptual reasons for which it is held, the way it reads or misreads the behavior of our mental concepts. In other words, the philosophical critic of this picture of the mind does not wish to dispute the fact that desire can numb people, that anger can drive them, that worry can give them duodenal ulcers, and that jealousy can be aroused by physical events. Nor does he wish to dispute the notion that, corresponding to every single quality of mind and character, there may be a physical or physiological counterpart in the body. What the philosophical critic wishes to examine is whether any of these facts or notions provides a reason for the physical picture of the mind as a chamber full of psychical entities that are interrelated in certain ways.

We have seen that underlying this theory of the mind are two conceptual assumptions. The first is that mental words necessarily name locatable entities, processes, events, occurrences, etc. The second is that the physical language that is used in talking about the mind is to be interpreted semi-literally, by analogy with its use in our talking about bodies.

The assumption that mental words necessarily name mental entities, processes, etc., is part of a more general assumption that every meaningful word names some particular thing or kind of thing. That assumption is mistaken. First, only an undue concentration on common nouns, such as "arm," "body," "man," etc., has obscured the obvious fact that many meaningful words do not refer to or name anything. There are in the world no ifs and ands, somes and notwithstandings, to which the so-called "syncategorematic" words, such as "if," "and," "some," and "notwithstanding" refer. Expressive words, like "bravo" and "damn," and evaluative words, like "good" and "beautiful," do not name anything. "Mouse" and "elephant" are used to refer to types of animals, but "large" does not refer to a property that a particular mouse and a particular elephant have in common; "large" indicates a relationship between this mouse and other mice, and between this elephant and other elephants. Even within the class of nouns, fictitious expressions like "centaur," and abstract nouns such as "justice," "truth," and "perfection" have a use other than to refer to some kind of object that exists somewhere. We have to find places in the world for repeated cases of what is called "blowing bubbles," but we do not have to find an extra place for what is called "the habit of blowing bubbles."

For our present purpose what we need to remember is that a word can have a meaning and therefore express a concept, without having to refer to some entity, process, or occurrence. Language, or thought, has more than one use. It was, indeed, the difficulty of finding the entity to which, on his own view of meaning, the word "mind" ought to refer that caused Hume such trouble in the eighteenth century. Further, we saw at the beginning of this chapter that it is so far an open question whether "mind" functions analogously to "body," or more as "British Constitution" does. It is equally so far an open question whether what are called "thoughts," "ideas," "desires," etc., have to be located in something, just because what are called "skin," "blood," "bones," etc., have to be so located.

It is worth mentioning here that the mistaken view about meaning discussed above is not confined to the words we use in discussing the mind. The beliefs in occult entities and qualities that were typical of some older science were largely due to the supposition that words like "force," "magnetism," "space," "time," etc., were used analogously to words like "body," "machine," and "combustion"—namely, to specify a kind of entity or process.

The second assumption that underlies the physical theory of the mind was that the physical metaphors used in our talk about the mind ought to be taken semi-literally, on close analogy with the use of the same words in our talk about the body. This assumption presses our analogies too far. To make it explicit is to cast doubt on it. There are many of these metaphors that no one is seriously tempted to take literally. "Deep," "shallow," "dirty," and "bright" do not refer to characteristics of minds that are in any way analogous to characteristics of cups and saucers. I do not have an idea literally in the back of my mind in the way in which I do have an important document at the back of my drawer, any more than I have a man's name literally on the tip of my tongue. Narrow-minded people are no more anatomical freaks than are big-hearted people. It will be part of my task in this book to show that it is equally, though perhaps more temptingly, mistaken to suppose that, for example, the acquisition of knowledge requires a mental storehouse analogous to a steel filing cabinet, or that the loss of a habit is analogous to the loss of an inhabitant. Locke was guilty of taking our metaphors too literally when he thought that describing the contents of one's mind was analogous to making an inventory of the contents of one's room.

The mistake of the physical theory is to suppose that there must exist psychical entities and processes, referred to by mental concepts, with sets of characteristics that are analogous to those that physical entities and processes, referred to by physical concepts, possess. But it would equally be a mistake to suppose that, since mental concepts are not used analogously to physical concepts, they should be abandoned altogether—to suppose, in short, that psychology should be replaced by physiology. We have to be equally careful of both the "Metaphysician's Mistake" and the "Physiologist's Fallacy." Both assume that to talk, for example, about a man's "ability" to do quadratic equations, or about his "habit" of criticizing others, is to speak of some entity or process in him. But, whereas the metaphysician says that an ability and a habit are mental entities or processes present in the mind—and that any physiological features of the brain can at most be their causes—the physiologist says that "ability" and "habit" refer solely to physical entities or processes in the brain, and that the alleged mental entities do not exist. Now each is right in what he denies, but wrong in what he affirms. To say of someone that he has such and such an ability or habit is to say something about his mind, not about his brain. It is not, however, to attribute to him a mental entity, process, or state; and there may be a physiological entity, process, or state that is causally necessary and sufficient for his having this ability or habit. The metaphysician and the physiologist are like two people both of whom assume that, "the capability of doing 100 m.p.h.," for example, is the name of some component under the hood of my car. While the metaphysician asserts that this capability is an immaterial component not visible to the mechanic, the physiologist says that it is only the special pistons. The physiologist is right in saying that the only components in the car are mechanical, but he is wrong in thinking that a car's capability is a mechanical component of the car. The metaphysician is right in insisting that its capability is not a mechanical component, but he is wrong in supposing that it is, therefore, a non-mechanical component. The assumption common to the metaphysician and the physiologist, the introspectionist and the behaviorist, is the product of a conceptual mistake.

The Freudian Theory

At the end of the nineteenth century, Freud began to make discoveries about the mind that revolutionized previous thinking. These discoveries and the theories founded on them are the concern of psychologists. What is of philosophical interest are those details of Freud's picture of the mind that are due, not to his observations or to experiments on his patients, but to the conceptual suppositions that shaped his thought. The absence of any necessary logical connection between his picture of the mind and his observations is confirmed by the fact that there are modern reformulations of his basic principles which conform with quite a different picture.

Freud's theory of mind is as much influenced as was that of any of his predecessors by the assumption that the meaning of a word is an object, or kind of object, that is named by the word. "Mind," he holds, is the name of a "psychical apparatus" that is divided into various "mental provinces," "agencies," "regions," or "systems," in which operate "energies" or "forces" that are called "instincts" and "ideas." The stated purpose of his last book, *An Outline of Psychoanalysis*, is to form "a general picture of the psychical apparatus, of the portions, organs and agencies of which it is composed, of the forces which operate in it, and of the functions which its different portions perform." The psychical apparatus is said to contain three "regions" ("realms," "provinces"), or "entities" or "formations," called the "Id," the "Ego," and the "Super-ego." The Id contains the inherited and fixed instincts. From it there arises the Ego, whose main task of self-preservation is accomplished partly by its becoming aware of external stimuli—which it proceeds to store, avoid, adapt, or modify—and partly by its controlling internal stimuli—that is, the instincts—either by satisfying them now or in the future or by suppressing them. Within this Ego, the Super-ego is formed by parental, social, and cultural influences.

There are similarities between Freud's tripartite division of the mind and Plato's. The Id, which "is directed exclusively to obtaining pleasure," corresponds fairly closely to Plato's element of desire, while the Ego and Super-ego share between them the tasks of Plato's spirited and ruling elements. Freud's picture of the Ego as a rider on the rebellious horse of the Id reminds us of Plato's charioteer. A closer parallel to Freud can, however, be found in Butler's eighteenth-century picture of the mind as a complex unit, composed of various appetites, or passions, and two reflective principles called "self-love" and "conscience." Freud's contrast between the Id's reckless pursuit of instinctive satisfactions and the Ego's concern to discover "the most favorable and least perilous method of obtaining satisfaction, taking the external world into account" is akin to Butler's contrast between the man who rashly rushes into danger for the sake of present gratification and the man who calmly and carefully pursues what his cool self-love advises him to be in his interests. Just as Freud's Super-ego "observes the Ego, gives it orders, corrects it and threatens it with punishments," so Butler's conscience, which is for him not the voice of our parents and our society but of God, is "a principle in man by which he approves or disapproves his heart, temper, and actions." Indeed, Freud occasionally calls the Super-ego an "ideal" Ego and explicitly equates it with conscience. Like Plato and Butler, Freud assumes that to say that a man loses his self-respect or becomes self-critical is to say that one part or agency of himself—i.e. his conscience—becomes the judge of another part of himself.

Freud sometimes said that his picture of the mind was based on experience and that he was only "translating into theory the results of observation." But it is clear that his theory was colored both by the political metaphors that had appealed to Plato and by the physical metaphors that had influenced psychologists from Descartes to his own day. Thus, Freud's interpretations of dreams and of abnormal behavior employ a picture of the mind as a rebellion-torn and conflict-ridden state in which the Id tries to "force its way into the Ego and into consciousness and in which the Ego arms itself afresh against the invasion." The Ego is pictured as a constitutional monarch or as a watchman who, by various indirect means, censors and represses unacceptable ideas. Alongside this analogy goes one based on the physical sciences. Although Freud declared in the early years of this century that he had abandoned his earlier hopes of solving psychological problems in terms of the brain rather than the mind, a brain-mind, or neurological-psychological, ambivalence characterizes all his work. The mind, like the brain, is described topographically: Id, Ego, and Super-ego are regions in a psychical apparatus. Sometimes Freud asserted that such a description, like the corresponding diagrams and pictures that he drew of the mind, was only a pictorial representation, which nevertheless might be near the truth, "an extensive approximation to the actual reality"; sometimes he said it was to be taken as an analogy. At times he held that, corresponding to the anatomy of the brain, there was a parallel landscape of the mind, while at other times he said that it was a purely terminological question whether his new concepts were to be taken physically or psychically. Usually, however, he categorically refused to identify the regions of the psychical apparatus with those of the physical, and insisted that "our psychical topography . . . has reference not to anatomical localities, but to regions in the mental apparatus, wherever they may be situated in the body."

The same ambivalence occurs in the details of his picture. Id, Ego, and Super-ego are entities to each of which, on the one hand, a "cortical layer" is assigned, while, on the other hand, they are referred to as systems and agencies in the psychical apparatus. The instincts are always described in terms of electrical forces and impulses, of energies, which are charged and displaced, excited and conserved. While sometimes they are called psychical representations of somatic forces, at other times they are equated with such forces, and are themselves psychically represented by ideas. The influence of the antithesis of attraction and repulsion in physics may partly account for Freud's fondness for dichotomous divisions—e.g., between cathexis and anticathexis, between the Thanatos (Death) and Eros (Love) instincts, or between pleasure and unpleasure.

Freud considered it to be a serious question whether or not we are to describe a situation in which we become conscious of some idea of which we were previously unconscious, in the "topographical" terms of the idea's moving from the locality of the Unconscious to that of the Preconscious or that of the Conscious, or in the "dynamic" terms of an addition or subtraction of energy to the idea. Often ideas from the Unconscious are pictured in "economic" terms as exerting pressure on the screen that has been raised between the Unconscious and the Conscious and Pre-conscious.

It is easy to see the purely conceptual moves that Freud made from the neutral description of his important factual discoveries to the mistaken picture of the mind that he thought these discoveries revealed. The discovery of how much we learn from experience and in our own general interest to check, modify, and adapt our immediate and natural desires by means of reflection and cool calculation is pictured as the elements of the Id coming under the control of the censorship of the Ego. Like Plato, Freud assumed that because a man, or his Ego, "can treat itself like any other object, observe itself, criticize itself, and do Heaven knows what besides with itself," therefore, "in such a case one part of the Ego stands over against the other . . . it splits when it performs many of its functions." The influence of family, social, and cultural standards and regulations on our early character is pictured as the growth of a third part of the mind, the Super-ego or conscience, which he insisted is a "genuine structural entity" and not a personified abstraction. Indecision, frustration, and anxiety are pictured as communal conflicts among these various "agencies" or their members.

Although I have insisted that this philosophical criticism of Freud's theory is not intended to throw any doubt on his epoch-making factual discoveries about the normal and abnormal behavior of human beings, we should not adopt the attitude that has become fashionable among some psychologists that it really does not matter how mistaken the theory is. Freud himself stressed that certain conceptual schemes may "correspond better to the real state of affairs," and warned of the danger that is inherent in taking literally inappropriate metaphors about the mind.

What, in Freud's view, chiefly distinguished his picture of the mind from that of his predecessors was the concept of the *Unconscious*. How did this notion arise? First, Freud made certain assumptions about the nature of explanation. He assumed that everything that happens has an explanation, i.e., nothing is of merely chance occurrence, and that every explanation is of the same type. It indicates an entity or process that immediately precedes the happening to be explained. Further, when what is to be explained is some normal or abnormal piece of human behavior of a "psychical" character—that is, when what is to be explained is an idea one gets, a conclusion one draws, a dream one has, a verbal slip one makes, some wish one cherishes, or an anxiety or obsession—then its cause is also "psychical." Since we are sometimes not aware or "conscious" of the alleged prior causes of our behavior, Freud concluded that there exist unconscious causes. In the last chapter of this book, I shall throw some doubt on these assumptions about the nature of explanation. Not all explanations imply the existence of antecedent processes. In particular it is a mistake—and Freud was guilty of this

—to suppose that an explanation of human conduct in terms of motives, or in terms of such feelings as envy, jealousy, and malice, is necessarily of this antecedent-event type. Reference to unconscious motives and feelings is not a reference to hidden antecedent entities, any more than reference to easily recognized motives and feelings is a reference to patent antecedent entities. This is not to deny that we often do things "unconsciously," or without knowing why we do them. I shall try later to provide an analysis of what we actually mean when we say this. Freud's view of causality appears also in his assumption that there can no more be gaps in a psychical series than in a physical series. Hence, where there seems to be a gap in the alleged psychical series, there must be an unconscious "missing link."

Secondly, Freud assumed—as did his predecessors—that ideas, wishes, feelings of love or hate, anxieties, and memories are psychical "objects," "processes," "acts," "activities," or "states" of one sort or another, of which we may be conscious very much as we may be conscious of a sound, a movement, or a man. The difference between himself and previous theorists, he insisted, was that he did not hold that psychical entities exist only when we are conscious of them; they can also exist, he believed, unknown to us. Hence, some of our thoughts and desires are repressed—that is, they are prevented from becoming known to us by being pressed back into the Unconscious. But, as I have already pointed out in my brief remarks above on *meaning*, it is a mistake to suppose that all words are the names of entities or sorts of entities, and I shall specifically show in later chapters that this is certainly a mistake in the case of "thoughts," "emotions," and "motives." We shall see that to realize that one loves or hates is not to inspect some psychical process called "love" or "hate"; neither is the failure to realize this, or the unwillingness to acknowledge it, to be explained by supposing that these processes are submerged in the depths of one's mind. The existence of desires of which we are unconscious, and feelings that we do not or cannot avow, even to our-

selves, is something with which we are familiar; but these
are not like hidden enemies, of whom we are unaware, or
secret files, whose existence we cannot admit. They are
more like drawings whose patterns we cannot make out, or
a wood we are unable to see for the trees.

Thirdly, Freud concluded that because, as he thought,
there exist in us entities and activities, such as ideas,
wishes, and feelings, of which we are unconscious, then
these psychical entities and activities exist in a part of the
psychical apparatus called "the Unconscious." He was
quite willing to acknowledge that for him "the word 'unconscious' has more and more been made to mean a mental
province rather than a quality which mental things have."
This is the same sort of false move as is made by those who
think that, because we often imagine things, our imagination is the abode of imaginary things: they take literally
the metaphorical saying, "It exists only in his imagination."

Fourthly, the Unconscious was thought to be needed as
the psychical place in which we store our knowledge and
our memories when we are not aware of them. "At any
given moment," said Freud, "consciousness includes only a
small content, so that the greater part of what we call conscious knowledge must in any case be for very considerable
periods of time in a state of latency, that is to say, of being
psychically unconscious. When all our latent memories are
taken into consideration it becomes totally incomprehen-
sible how the existence of the unconscious can be denied."
In 1916 he insisted that " 'Unconscious' is no longer a
term for what is temporarily latent; the unconscious is a
special realm, with its own desires and modes of experience and peculiar mental mechanisms not elsewhere opera-
tive." Easily recallable knowledge and memories were said
to be stored in the Pre-conscious; the rest was sunk more
deeply in the Unconscious.

This assumption—that our acquired knowledge needs a
mental storehouse, in the same way that our written information needs a filing cabinet—is a mistake about the
concept of *knowledge* that is based on a false analogy, as

old as Plato's simile of the aviary in his *Theaetetus*, between the acquisition of knowledge and the acquisition of material possessions. To have a store of knowledge is to have the ability to reproduce certain correct answers, not to possess a collection of psychical pieces of information; just as to have a trait of character, such as conceit, or a habit, perhaps of dropping one's aspirates, is to have a tendency to behave in certain ways, not a psychical entity or formation. A motor-car has a place under its hood for the special pistons that give it the capability of doing 100 m.p.h.; it does not have another place for the capability itself, which is not at present being exercised. Similarly, our heads contain the physiological equipment for us to reproduce the information that we acquire; they do not contain another, psychical, place where the information itself is stored. Because acquiring knowledge, or traits, or habits, is not thus analogous to acquiring material possessions, the ability to produce our knowledge, or the tendency to manifest our traits and our habits, does not imply the existence of a place in which the as yet unproduced knowledge, or unmanifested traits and habits, is kept—in the way that the ability to produce a notebook does imply the existence of a place in which the notebook is kept when it is not in use. There is no more an answer to the question "Where is my knowledge when I am not recalling it?" than there is to the question "Where is my conceit when I am not displaying it?" Whether or not I am always, or ever, conscious of my habit of dropping my aspirates, it is a mistake to suppose that, when that habit is not at work, it has either disappeared or is being kept hidden in some place, perhaps a psychical place.

Freud's unwillingness to accept such an analysis of latent knowledge was based on his view that knowledge and memory are "psychical processes." If consciously recalling a scene of childhood is to be allowed as a mental process, he thought that it was mere prejudice to insist on a purely physical explanation of stored or unconscious memories. He had moved so far from his early scientific studies, in

short, that he now avoided the physiologist's fallacy only
to fall into the metaphysician's mistake.

The Functional Theory

The Political, the Physical, and the Freudian theories of
the mind all share the assumption that we employ the
concept of *mind* and other mental concepts in order to
think and talk about some kinds of entities and occurrences that are related in various ways to the physical
entities and occurrences that we call "bodily." Quite different from these is a theory, proposed originally by Aristotle and resurrected in twentieth-century psychology and
philosophy, according to which "mind" is not the name of
a particular entity, but indicates an organized set of functions (e.g. thinking and feeling), dispositions (e.g. patience and irritability), and abilities (e.g. to solve problems or to remember facts), that are manifested in human,
and perhaps in animal, behavior. Further, this theory holds
that to describe a particular piece of behavior in "mental"
terms is not to refer to a prior occurrence or entity that
was its cause, nor to the particular constituents of which
it is composed, but to certain features of its character, its
manner, its purpose, its procedure, or its classification.
Such a theory I shall call the "Functional" theory of the
mind. I shall exemplify it from the writings of Aristotle, of
several twentieth-century psychologists, and of the contemporary English philosopher, Gilbert Ryle.

ARISTOTLE

It is not to be expected that Aristotle should altogether
have escaped the assumption of his and later times that
nouns such as "mind" and "soul" name entities. Some of
his questions about the nature of what he called the
"psyche," together with an explicit hesitancy as to whether
one can properly, in some sense, speak of "parts" of the
psyche, and a few obscure remarks about the possible in-

destructibility of one of these "parts," show the influence of this assumption.

But in general Aristotle is sharply distinguished from most other theorists of the mind by his advocacy of what I am calling the "Functional" view. His view stems primarily from his doctrine of definition—namely, that to ask of anything "What is it?" is to ask for its "essence," and this is to ask for its "function." An axe is not something made of wood and iron, it is something used for cutting. An eye is not an object of such and such shape and color —unless you are referring to an eye in the derivative sense, in which a painted eye or a stone eye is also an eye; it is something that has the power of sight. A flute is not an instrument of a specified shape, but one with the function of producing certain musical notes. Plants, animals, and men are logically identifiable, not by their physical properties, but by their functions and powers. Things are what they are capable of doing. To lose one's function is to lose one's identity.

Another name that is given to this functionally defined essence is "form." When we say of any particular thing that it is a certain material, e.g. stone, metal, or tissue, that is employable for a certain end, we say that it has matter and form. The form of an instrument is its work; of an axe, the power to cut; of an eye, the ability to see. In describing a living thing, we call its matter "body" and its form "psyche."

Since each thing is defined in terms of its form, one kind of living thing, e.g. a plant, is distinguished from another, e.g. a man, by attributing to it a different kind of psyche. Its psyche makes it what it is. But to attribute any kind of psyche to something is to describe its functions and powers. For instance, to say that the divided parts of a plant or a worm continue to have the same psyche as the original organism is to say that they retain the same capacities. To destroy anything's psyche is to deprive it of its identity as an organism capable of doing such and such.

Aristotle proceeds to distinguish living things into plants,

which have the power to absorb nourishment and to reproduce; animals, which have these powers together with a
tendency to desire things and an ability to feel and dis-
criminate by some of the five senses; and men, who in
addition to the nutritive and reproductive powers of plants
and the sentient powers of animals have the ability to
think. To say that a man has a rational psyche is to say
that he possesses the power of thought as well as the sentient, nutritive, and reproductive powers of lower forms of
life. To distinguish "mind" from "soul" is merely to distinguish the power to think from the other powers of a
living organism.

For Aristotle, therefore, to call anything a human being
is to say that it is a piece of matter, which may be called
a "body," of a certain form—that is, with a certain set of
functions—which may be called its "psyche." A psyche,
whether of a plant, an animal, or a man, is not a sort of
immaterial body, which either survives or dies with the
material body and which may have one or many parts.
It is the set of functions by virtue of which we identify
the body that has it as being that of a plant, an animal,
or a man. To explain any piece of behavior by referring to
the psyche is, for Aristotle, not to explain the behavior as
the effect of an inner object, but as the exercise of a capacity or the manifestation of a disposition. To possess a trait
of character, such as honesty or temperance, or to possess
some knowledge, is to have a tendency or an ability to
behave in certain ways. It is not to retain any sort of material in a place called the "mind," or the "psyche."

We can see how Aristotle's theory of the psyche depends
on his philosophical theory of definition. Without subscrib-
ing entirely to the view that all classificatory or identifying
words signify the function that something performs, rather
than any other properties it has, we may agree with him
that this is true of many mental concepts. Such classificatory words as "slave," "engineer," "monkey," "knife," and
"man," as well as "mind," "intelligence," "will," "memory,"
and "knowledge," may refer to functions, tendencies, and

capabilities, even though "apple," "mountain," and "circle" do not.

TWENTIETH CENTURY PSYCHOLOGY

The early years of this century saw the rise of the Functional view in psychology. It substituted a study of mental operations and activities for the study of mental constituents and their combinations, and preferred an examination of the functions of the mind to an examination of its constitution or structure. Further, it was not the contents of mental operations and activities that were of interest, but rather their manner and purpose. The mind was regarded, not as a container of various simple and complex elements, combined and separated by the influence of different forces, which caused a man to behave in such and such a manner, but partly as a set of various human activities performed in a certain manner and for a certain purpose, and partly as a set of dispositions and capabilities of which these activities are the manifestations. While Freud in 1915 still thought that a place in the mind was needed, in order to store our acquired but unused knowledge, William McDougall had said in 1912 that such knowledge is constituted by "the total system formed by the cognitive dispositions of the mind."

Although the Functional view was conceded to be as old as Aristotle, its revival at the beginning of this century was due partly to a transfer of affection on the part of psychologists from physics to biology. Just as the zoologists suggested that organisms should be studied in terms of their functions, their capabilities and their habits, rather than their structure—in terms of what they do rather than what they are like—so the psychologists pointed out that what constitutes a mental operation, such as thinking of X, remembering Y, or having an idea of Z, is not a set of contents but a type of function. We say of someone that he had the same thought on two occasions, not because of an identity of the elements that were present on the two occasions—whether these be images or sensations—but because of an identity in the functioning of whatever elements were present. "We may never have twice," said Angell in 1907, "exactly the same idea viewed from the side of sensuous structure and composition. But there seems nothing whatever to prevent our having, as often as we will, contents of consciousness which mean the same thing. They function in one and the same practical way, however discrepant their momentary texture. The situation is rudely analogous to the biological case where very different structures may under different conditions be called on to perform identical functions." We may, as Wittgenstein did later, regard an idea by analogy with a chess piece, which is identified by its function and not by its shape, and a mental operation by analogy with a chess move, which is identified by its relation to the rules of the game and not by a spatial position on a particular board.

McDougall and Tolman are two psychologists who followed Aristotle in stressing that it is the similarity in the manner and circumstances of various movements, rather than the similarity of the actual movements themselves, that constitutes the various sets of movements as the same action. A hallmark of "mental" activity, they agree with him, is its purposiveness—that is, its goal-seeking character.

From the biologists' study of animals, psychologists had acquired the notions of function and purposiveness; from their own study of animals they learned, like Aristotle, not only to appreciate the similarity between animal and human behavior, but also how much could be discovered about behavior without relying on the method of introspection. Why, they asked in contrast to Descartes, should behavioral concepts not be used in the same way about men and animals?

Another formative influence on the views of some Functionalists was Pragmatism, the philosophy of meaning and truth that was characteristic of late nineteenth-century American thought; it insists on defining terms by reference to conditional consequences. According to Pragmatism, to say, for example, that a diamond is "hard" is to say that, if you rub it against another substance, it scratches rather than is scratched; to talk about the "force" of so and so is to talk about its pressure effects. Functionalists like McDougall maintained that previous theorists of mind had wrongly "reified" mental concepts that were really dispositional. That is, they had thought that "mind" refers to an entity, when in fact it is used to speak of a set of dispositions. The structure of the mind, McDougall held, should be likened, not to the structure of a piece of machinery, with its pieces spatially related, but to the structure of a play.

From 1901 to 1909 the Wurzburg School of psychologists tried without success to find by introspection the "contents" of thoughts and the "acts of judgment" that were presupposed by the current physical and chemical models of the mind. Such failure suggested that there might have been a fundamentally wrong approach to the nature of thought and judgment. Even such an opponent of Functionalism as Titchener seems to have been aware of the significance of the linguistic fact that many mental concepts, such as *recognition, imagination, conception, judgment,* and *attention,* are expressed by verbal nouns, which refer to the functions a person performs, rather than by nouns such as "idea" and "thought," which seem to refer to objects that he possesses. McDougall said, "My thinking of the horse is not the bringing out into the light the consciousness of some entity that had been lying stored in some dark pigeon-hole of the mind; it was rather an exercise of the faculty of knowing determined and directed by the activity of a complex of mental dispositions."

It would seem, therefore, that the change from one theory of the mind to another, even on the part of empirical psychologists, came about largely because of analogies— now biological ones, instead of physical and chemical ones; because of problems of verification—how one tests whether a man or an animal feels, thinks, remembers, or is conscious; and because of conceptual considerations—is the identity of a piece of thinking or of a wish constituted by

its content or by its character? Is a demonstration of knowledge like the exercise of an ability, or is it like the effect of
a cause?

TWENTIETH CENTURY PHILOSOPHY

The best contemporary philosophical representatives of
the Functional theory of the mind are Ryle and Wittgenstein. Let us look at Ryle's *The Concept of Mind,* which
appeared in 1949. As a philosophical theory it is, of course,
based on purely conceptual considerations—that is, on an
examination of the ways in which our everyday mental
concepts are actually used.

The negative side of this theory is a revolt against the
mistaken theory of meaning that regards every word as
the name of some sort of entity or occurrence. " 'Mind',"
Ryle holds, "is not the name of another person, working or
frolicking behind an impenetrable screen; it is not the
name of another place . . . it is not the name of another
tool . . . or another appliance . . ."; nor is it the name
"of a second theatre of special-status incidents." The positive thesis is that the word "mind" is used analogously to
"British Constitution," for example, which refers to the
ways in which various other things—such as Sovereign,
Parliament, the Church, the Judicature and the laws—are
related together. To describe a person's mind as brilliant
or dull, quick or slow, honest or dirty is not to refer to
some inner entity that causes him to act in certain ways,
but rather to his abilities and tendencies to act in such
ways. "The traditional theory of the mind," says Ryle, "has
misconstrued the type-distinction between disposition and
exercise into its mythical bifurcation of unwitnessable
mental causes and their witnessable physical effects."
Hence, self-knowledge is not to be obtained by intro-
specting these alleged mental causes.

The theory that "mind" is the name of an entity was,
as we saw, partly due to the supposed necessity of finding
a repository for such alleged objects as ideas, thoughts,
knowledge, images, memories, and feelings. Therefore, the

Functional attack on this theory is backed up by smaller-scale attacks on the supposition that these mental concepts do refer to such objects. Ryle tries to show that to say that someone has an idea is not to imply that there is some entity called an "idea," which needs to be kept somewhere, in the way in which our material possessions need to be kept. Having an idea or a theory is "being prepared to make a variety of moves." Similarly, the person who feels a twinge, an inclination or a desire, or who feels in a certain mood, does not need a mental box in which the twinges, inclinations and desires may exist, in the way in which he needs a physical box for the toothbrushes and the inkwells that he can also "feel." Desires are not internal occurrences, which their owner either witnesses or fails to witness, nor are motives, whether hidden or obvious, antecedent causes of his behavior. Therefore, no places labeled "the Conscious" and "the Unconscious" need to be provided for their abode. "Imagination" and "memory" are not the names of parts of something called "mind," in which are stored the things that a day-dreamer "sees" or a madman "hears." "Much as stage-murders do not have victims and are not murders, so seeing things in one's mind's eye does not involve either the existence of things seen or the occurrence of acts of seeing them. So no asylum is required for them to exist or occur in." The man who dwells in memory or imagination on the scenes of his childhood is not, according to Ryle, "being a spectator of a resemblance of his nursery, but he is resembling a spectator of his nursery." Finally, I have already shown briefly that having an ability, a habit, or a good deal of knowledge, unlike having an apple, a hat, or a good deal of cash, does not involve the existence of a mental or physical place in which to keep them.

As a result of detailed examinations of these various particular mental concepts, the Functional theory concludes that "to talk of a person's mind is not to talk of a repository which is permitted to house objects that something called 'the physical world' is forbidden to house; it is to talk of the person's abilities, liabilities and inclinations to do and undergo certain sorts of things, and of the doing and undergoing of these things in the ordinary world."

As with *mind*, so with *will, intellect, Ego,* etc., Ryle tries "to refute the doctrine that there exists a Faculty, Immaterial Organ or Ministry corresponding to the (physical) theory's description of the 'Will' and, accordingly, that there occur processes or operations, corresponding to what it describes as 'volitions.' " On the contrary, "strength of will is a propensity the exercises of which consist in sticking to tasks . . . weakness of will is having too little of this propensity." "Intellect," "Understanding," and "Reason" are not the names of mental organs or lecturers. Nor is "I" the proper name of an inner part of ourselves, any more than "now" is the name of a particular moment in time.

A careful insistence on the manifold variety of concepts provides Ryle with another line of attack against theories of mind that think of it as a kind of entity. First, I have already mentioned that many of the words that we use to characterize people signify abilities, tendencies, or liabilities, and not activities, occurrences, acts, or entities. Secondly, among words that do signify occurrences, there is a very important class that is used to report success or failure in the performance of a task, rather than to report the performance itself. "Convince," "prove," "conclude," "deduce," "discover," and "solve" all have an importance in our talk about the mind, but these verbs do not refer to activities going on inside a mental chamber, because they do not refer to activities going on at all. Thirdly, Ryle argues that there is a large class of descriptions of human activities that has been traditionally misconstrued as if its members were simple descriptions of several incidents, at least one of which takes place in the mind, when really they are complex descriptions of a single incident, which does not take place in the mind. For instance, just as a bird who, by flying south at a certain time of the year, is thereby migrating, does not do two things, so a musician —who plays the piano and thereby obeys an order—or a driver—who keeps to his own side of the road and thereby takes care—does not, in Ryle's view, do two things, one physical and the other mental. Each is doing one thing in a certain manner, in certain circumstances, or for a certain reason. Such complex descriptions of one overt piece of behavior, which are mistakenly construed as simple descriptions of one overt together with one inner piece of behavior, Ryle calls "semi-hypothetical," or "mongrel-categorical," statements. We shall see in later chapters their ubiquity in our language about the mind.

In short, the Functional theory regards mental concepts, not as referring to mysterious inner entities and processes that affect our outward behavior, but as a way of referring to certain characteristics of that behavior. "The styles and procedures of people's activities," says Ryle, "*are* the way their minds work and are not merely imperfect reflections of the postulated secret processes which were supposed to be the workings of minds."

Enough should now have been said to enable the reader to see in broad outline the conceptual considerations on which the Functional theory of the mind, whether in Aristotle or in contemporary psychology and philosophy, is founded. Since this theory, especially in its contemporary philosophical form, seems to me to be much nearer the truth than any of its rivals, it will be most convenient to leave criticisms of it to my ensuing detailed discussions of particular mental concepts. To these I now turn.

CHAPTER 3

Attention

Different Kinds of Attention-Concepts

In our everyday thinking we use a set of concepts that in different ways involve the notion of *attention*. We cannot take an *interest* in or *enjoy* or *think* about something without giving it at least momentary attention; *awareness*, *consciousness* and *noticing* are all closely related to this notion. To behave carelessly, inadvertently or absent-mindedly is to act, in different ways, without attention. Lawyers are concerned with the notion of *negligence*, social psychologists employ interest-scales, *consciousness* has provided a stumbling block for behaviorist psychology, and *enjoyment* is a central concept in aesthetics.

Although all these notions involve that of *attention*, the notion of *attention* involves some of them not at all and others only to a degree. The closest attention is possible without either interest or enjoyment; a man may be completely absorbed in something, even though he is not taking any care. Although one cannot be said to notice something if it has not attracted any part of one's attention, there can well be features of the object of attention that one does not notice. When one attends to X—e.g., a book —although there must be some description of X, e.g. as a book, under which it is true that one is aware of X or realizes that it is X, yet it is not merely possible, but quite common, that one does not realize, in paying attention to X, that one is paying attention to Y—e.g., a first edition of James Joyce. In other words, there is a sense in which "He did not realize what he was paying attention to" may be true and also a sense in which it is necessarily false.

All these concepts of attention share three important characteristics. First, they all demand an object. It makes no sense to speak of someone as merely "enjoying" or "taking care," or "being interested"; his enjoyment, his care or his interest—like his attention, his thought, and his awareness—must have an object. Secondly, while we can adequately describe the process of crying or smiling without mentioning what we are crying or smiling about, we cannot adequately describe the process of paying attention without referring to the object of our attention, any more than we can adequately describe what happens in expectation or wishing without referring to their objects. The specific character of an instance of attending, like that of expecting but unlike that of smiling, depends on its object. A careful engine-driver differs from a careful surgeon in what he does. Thirdly, one cannot give one's attention in any way to anything without knowing that one is attending, and also knowing, under some description, what one is attending to. Thus, we cannot say that someone is doubtful whether he is pleased at or thinking about anything, or that he is doubtful what it is that he is pleased at or thinking about.

These three characteristics of attention-concepts are also possessed by such notions as *hope, fear, expectation,* and *wishing.* For example, expectation must have an object; descriptions of expectation differ according to what there is expectation of; one cannot expect something without knowing that and what one is expecting. Notions such as *fear* and *expectation* also have a fourth characteristic— namely, that the objects of what they signify need not exist, except in one's fear or expectation; so that one may expect what will never happen, or fear a creature of one's own imagination. This characteristic is sometimes called "intentionality." Attention-concepts, however—with the exception of *thinking*—are not "intentional." If the triumph that one enjoys is only in one's imagination, then one does not strictly speaking enjoy a triumph, but only the thought of one; one cannot be conscious of a disability that one does not in fact possess.

A further characteristic that attention-concepts share with one another and with many other mental concepts, such as *fear*, *hope* and *expectation*, is that of being "poly-morphous."

Following Ryle ("Thinking and Language" in *Proceedings of the Aristotelian Society*, Suppl. XXV (1951), pp. 67–69), we may distinguish between a specific concept, such as *singing*, *presenting arms*, or *counting*, and a poly-morphous concept, such as *working*, *practicing*, or *obeying*. A concept X is polymorphous—that is, one that takes many forms—if there are many different things one or another of which can in certain circumstances count as X, and yet none of which in other circumstances necessarily counts as X. It is the second of these two conditions that dis-tinguishes a polymorphous concept, such as *obedience*, from a generic concept, such as *perception*. Neither a polymorphous nor a generic concept is limited to one form or to one species; the generic concept of *perceiving* has the species of *seeing* and *hearing* as well as that of *smelling*, and the polymorphous concept of *obeying* can have the forms of *presenting arms* and *singing* as well as that of *counting*. On the other hand, a species necessarily implies its genus, whereas that form which a polymorphous concept takes on one occasion need not on another occasion be a form of this same, or perhaps of any other, poly-morphous concept. Thus, since I perceive by seeing or hearing, I cannot do either of these without perceiving; but, even though I can obey by presenting arms, by sing-ing, or by counting, I could do any or all of these things without thereby obeying any order. What makes "obeying" a true or false description of my presenting arms or of my singing is not anything in these specific actions themselves, but in the circumstances of their performance. Any word that expresses a polymorphous concept does not name some specific thing; it indicates the relationship of that thing to its circumstances, and thereby signifies what, on this occasion, it is a form of.

A very simple example of a polymorphous concept is the concept of *repetition*. What makes anything a repetition cannot be any feature that is peculiar to the specific thing done. For, first, anything whatsoever, if it is done for the second time, is a repetition, and nothing whatsoever, if it is done for the first time, is a repetition. Secondly, whatever counts as a repetition of X cannot in itself differ from X. What makes "repetition" a true description of anything is the circumstances in which it is done—namely, that it has been done before.

All attention-concepts are, like the concepts of *obedience* and *repetition*, polymorphous. First, simply to say that someone is in any way attentive gives us no more clue as to what specifically he is doing or undergoing than to say that he is repeating himself. We show our interest in music, our consciousness of our responsibilities, or our care in proofreading, in quite different ways from those in which we show our interest in philosophy, our consciousness of class, or our care in driving a car, just as what we do in repeating one action is quite different from what we do in repeating another action. Secondly, we could be doing the sorts of things that on other occasions would indicate our interest, consciousness, or care, even though they do not do so on this occasion, just as we could be doing for the first time the sort of thing that, if it were done for the second time, would amount to a repetition. Not all attendance at lectures is a sign of interest, nor is a clear and slow enunciation necessarily an exercise of care in speech. Thirdly, we attend, just as we repeat or obey, by doing or undergoing something else, such as looking, listening, or keeping quiet. We could ask someone either to look, to listen, *or* to keep quiet, just as we could ask him to read, to write, *or* to sing; but we could not sensibly ask him to look, listen, *or* attend, any more than we could sensibly ask him to read, write *or* obey. We should have to ask him to look, listen, or *in some other way* attend; to read, write, or *in some other way* obey. Attention, like obedience, takes different forms; it is not an alternative to these forms. Finally, the features that we pay attention to, take an interest in, notice, or are conscious of, are not additional to those that we encounter in things by using our senses and our intellect. Sights, sounds, smells, tastes, and feelings are the peculiar objects of the senses just as, perhaps, thoughts are of the intellect; but there are no objects that are peculiar to attention, interest, and consciousness.

There are important differences between individual attention-concepts. Primarily, as we shall see, they differ in their relation to *attention* itself. What we attend to is what we pay attention to, while what we are interested in is what we are inclined to pay attention to. Care consists in the attention we pay to the risks in what we do. We notice what captures our attention, we are conscious of what holds it. Secondly, attention-concepts differ in their range. We can pay attention to, take an interest in, or think about almost any object or characteristic, as well as any activities and feelings on the part of ourselves and others. We can, on the other hand, be careful only in what we ourselves do, and we can enjoy only what affects ourselves. Thirdly, attention-concepts differ in that they qualify different aspects of what we do. They may, like *absent-minded* and *inadvertent,* indicate inattention to the deed itself; or, like *mechanical* and *inattentive,* to its mode of procedure; or, like *automatic* and *impulsive,* to its preparation; or, like *careless* and *thoughtless,* to its effects; or, like *regardless,* to its circumstances.

Cutting across this third difference is a fourth—namely, the difference between the use of an attention-concept to describe the manner in which something is done and its use to provide an explanation of its being done. This difference, which is characteristic of many attention-concepts, is often indicated in English by the position of the attention-word, either after or before the verb that signifies the deed. Thus, to say that a man drove carefully, wandered about absent-mindedly, or read a book with interest, is to describe the *manner* in which he did these things. To say, on the other hand, that he carefully kept to the left of the road, absent-mindedly put his foot in a puddle, or read a book from interest, is to give an *explanation* for his performance of these deeds. Some attention-concepts, such as *inadvertently* or *automatically*, can be used only to provide an explanation of what we do, as when we inadvertently let out a secret or automatically answer "no"; others, such as *mechanically*, can signify only the manner in which we act.

When an attention-concept furnishes an explanation of something we do, it does so, not by giving the cause of which our deed was the effect, but by referring to the polymorphous activity that took the form of this specific deed: just as to explain a soldier's presenting arms in terms of his obedience to an order is a matter of relating his specific deed to its polymorph, not to its antecedent cause. Thus, a deed or omission that is explicable by our carelessness or absent-mindedness is a careless or absent-minded deed or omission. It is a piece of carelessness or absent-mindedness, just as acts that are due to obedience are obedient acts. Our deed is not the *effect* of our carelessness. On the other hand, the pedestrian's death that is due to our carelessness in not using our headlights is an effect, of which our carelessness is the cause. We can say either that our carelessness or that our failure to use our headlights was the cause of the pedestrian's death. Therefore, the relation between our carelessness and our failure to use our headlights cannot be the same as the relation between our carelessness and the pedestrian's death. Indeed, while our carelessness might, fortunately, have no effects, it could not be without specific instances.

When a polymorphous concept, such as *obedience, practice, attention,* or *care,* is used to make an explanatory statement, then the whole statement has a complex function. It is at once narrative, explanatory, and conditionally predictive. Consider a man who is playing the piano for practice—that is, practicing on the piano. He is both practicing and playing the piano, although he is not doing two things at once, like a man who is playing the piano with a smile. His playing is his practicing; he practices by playing. Further, he is playing the piano because he is practicing; hence, we could predict the sorts of things he would do in certain circumstances—e.g., repeat a piece until he had improved his performance. In a similar way, a man who is carefully underlining every foreign word on a page is both underlining foreign words and taking care, although he is not doing two things at once, as would be a man who is underlining foreign words and crossing out English words. It would be a mistake to look, perhaps in his mind, for the exercise of care, in addition to the physical act of crossing out, just as it would be to look for the practicing in addition to the piano playing; but it would not be a mistake to look for the smile as well as the piano playing. The reader's underlining is on this occasion his taking care; he exercises his care by underlining. Further, he is underlining the foreign words because he is taking care, perhaps to edit his manuscript, and hence we could predict what he would do in certain other circumstances. A statement whose function is to give such a logically complex account of a particular deed, rather than a particular account of a complex of deeds, has been called by Ryle (*The Concept of Mind*, 1949, pp. 135–49) a "mongrel-categorical" statement. Such statements play a large part in everyday discourse, especially in what we say about the mind.

It is, however, a mistake to suppose that attention-concepts necessarily form mongrel-categorical statements. They do so only in their explanatory use. A host who attentively passes his guest the cheese manifests his attention by passing it. His attention to his guest's needs explains his passing it, and allows us to predict the likelihood of other signs of attention. But a man who plays the piano attentively does not manifest his attention by playing the piano; he does not play because he is attending. In a similar way, a motorist who carefully sounds his horn at a turn in the road shows his care in driving by sounding his horn; he sounds it because he is taking care. A man who is driving carefully along the road, on the other hand, takes care in doing this, not *by* doing it. He is not driving along the road because he is taking care in driving. Hence, the statements "He attentively passed the cheese" and "He carefully sounded his horn," like "He is playing the piano for practice," are mongrel-categorical statements, whereas "He is playing the piano attentively" and "He drove carefully along the road," like "He played the piano smilingly," are not.

So much for some of the general characteristics of attention-concepts. Let us now turn to consider some specific examples of such concepts.

Attending

We may attend—that is, give or pay attention—to almost anything; to a physical object or a person or to any characteristic of these, to a situation or event, a problem or controversy, to our own activity or that of someone else, or to some feeling that we have. When we attend to what is past—e.g. look at a distant star or listen to distant guns —or to what is future—e.g. prepare for next week's wedding—we must attend also to something present connected with the past or future—e.g. to the appearance of the star or the sound of the guns, or to the preparations for the wedding. Or else we can think about the past and the future.

Whatever its object, *attending* has the logical characteristics of an activity-concept—that is, it applies to something we do or are engaged in. Like any activity, attending takes time; it can be intermittent or continuous, interrupted or uninterrupted. Hence, the verb takes such continuous forms as "I am attending" and "He was not paying attention." Attending has a certain manner: perfunctory or intent, reluctant or conscientious, calm or excited, careful or not very careful. Unlike some activities, however, it cannot be qualified by reference to its method or its objective; we do not give our attention thoroughly or unsystematically, methodically or haphazardly, successfully or unsuccessfully. Attending is not a form of searching; it is like looking *at* or listening *to*, rather than looking *for* or listening *for*. The only instance in which one can be described as "systematically" attending to or looking at something occurs when one attends to or looks at various parts of it in a certain order; but one cannot speak of each separate part being attended to either systematically or unsystematically.

One may attend, as one may do many things, for a particular purpose, but attending, unlike searching, need not be done on purpose. We can attend to something, just as we can look at it, solely for pleasure, or because, being fascinated, we simply cannot take our attention away from it. This is one important difference between the attention that we pay in merely attending and that which we pay in taking care; the latter sort of attention must have a purpose. Whether or not it is done on purpose, attending, like any other activity, may either have or fail to have a result. One job of the phrases "to notice" and "to fail to notice" is to signify this result or lack of result.

To pay attention is something one can decide or resolve or promise or refuse to do; hence, it is something we can blame someone for not doing. We can train someone to attend, just as we train him to acquire any habit; attending is something we may do either willingly or unwillingly. Normally, we "give" or "pay" attention, or even "direct" or "turn" our attention to something. In casual behavior we "lend," or "let someone have," our attention; when we are earnest or steadfast, we "focus" or "glue" it. Unwilling or unpremeditated attention is said to be "attracted," "arrested," "seized"; when fascinated, we "cannot take our attention off" the object.

Attending is not, however, a specific activity. Being polymorphous, it is something that manifests itself in one or another of a range of activities. "Attending" characterizes certain of our activities in a specific way, rather than naming a specific activity. We pay attention by doing something specific, such as looking, listening, studying, or writing. What makes these, or any other activities, instances of paying attention is that, when we do them, something is made the center, or object, or topic in regard to which we are actively busy or occupied in these perceptual, intellectual, or practical ways. Attention is something we can focus, concentrate, or center on an object. To give one's attention to one's philosophy involves reading books, doing essays, going to lectures, and in other ways spending time on the subject. To pay attention to one's handwriting is to make it the object of one's efforts. One might be engaged in any of these activities under circumstances such that, say, the philosophy or the handwriting was not their center; they would not then count as forms of paying attention to one's philosophy or one's handwriting. Because one focuses on what is perceptible by using the appropriate sense-faculty, and on what is intelligible by making it the object of one's thinking, the general notion of *attention* can be specified in terms of these particular perceptual and intellectual activities. Thus, we can "attend to" or "look at" the blackboard, "attend to" or "listen to" the music; we ask someone to give us his attention or to lend us his ears, we catch the waiter's attention or his eye; to be the cynosure of all eyes is to be the center of attention. We can give a good deal of thought or attention to a request, and our mind or our attention may be fixed on or engaged by a knotty problem.

When the object of one's attention is one's own activity —that is, when one is said to "attend to what one is doing"—it is important to distinguish between attending as a spectator and attending as an agent. If I attend as a spectator to what I am doing, then I attend to what I am doing in the way in which I attend either to what someone else is doing or to something other than an activity. The learner-driver watches his own driving as he watches his instructor's. But to attend in this way to one's driving is not necessarily to drive attentively. If, on the other hand, I attend as an agent to what I am doing, I do what I am doing attentively. I cannot attend as an agent to what someone else is doing because his doing it cannot also be my own attentive doing of it. The accomplished driver attends to his driving by driving attentively, not by watching himself as he drives.

To attend as a spectator to what one is doing is to make this activity itself the direct object of one's study. To attend as an agent to what one is doing is to occupy oneself with various tasks that are relevant to one's main activity, and to keep oneself disengaged from tasks that are irrelevant to it. The writer on the art of fishing attends to his fishing by watching what he does when he is fishing. The attentive fisherman, on the other hand, is distinguished from the inattentive fisherman by the fact that he keeps his eyes on the water, his ears open for the rustling of the reeds, and his mind on the habits of fish, instead of looking at his watch, listening to the airplane, or worrying about his stocks and shares.

Notice

The sorts of things that can be noticed are in the main those to which attention can be paid—that is, present perceptual and intellectual objects, the activities of ourselves and others, and certain kinds of feeling.

Noticing is not an activity. The verb "to notice" does not have either a present continuous ("am noticing") or a past habitual ("was noticing") tense, because noticing is not something in which one can be engaged for a period of time. Noticing in students' essays the mistaken use of "criteria" as a singular noun is something I can do continually, but not continuously. Noticing does not occupy any time, although time may elapse before I notice something. It is not something that has a manner or a method. To ask why someone noticed something is to ask how it was that he came to notice it. To ask why he attended to it is to ask his reason for paying attention. On the other hand, while we can ask how someone noticed something, we cannot, in this same sense, ask how he attended to it. To ask what made me notice X is to ask what it was about the features of X, such as its size, position or novelty, that struck me or drew my attention to it. To ask what made me attend to X is to seek an answer in terms of such things as interest, curiosity, duty, chance, or purpose. Quickness or slowness to notice things shows aptitude; speed in attending is the measure of willingness, interest, fear, etc. Criticism for failure to notice casts doubt on one's preparedness to receive what was available; it may be a disparagement of one's intellect, or sensory capacity, or knowledge—or it may be a hint that one was simply not attending. Blame for failure of attention is usually a reflection on one's character. Apologies may always be demanded for inattention, but apologies for failure to notice, only when this was due to inattention. Training that is designed to improve one's likelihood of noticing things is meant to improve aptitude and knowledge, not to overcome the natural inclinations of the inattentive. It is because "attend" signifies something we do and "notice" something we receive, that only the latter can be followed, in a statement, by reference to what has been gotten. We can notice that something has happened, or how or whether or when or where it happened; but we cannot attend to these. To pretend not to notice is to try to conceal something that has been received; not, as with pretending not to be attending, to hide the fact that we were doing something. The natural marks of attention—the knitted brow, the puzzled face, the intent pose—are marks of the search for an answer; by contrast, the signs that someone has noticed—the sudden tension or relaxation, the consequent changes in behavior—suggest that the answer has come.

We cannot advise, request, or encourage someone to notice, as we can advise, etc. him to take note; noticing is not something one can decide, agree, or refuse to do. Some things we cannot help noticing, others are easy not to notice; but we cannot notice willingly or against our will.

Recognition of the logical features of *noticing* so far mentioned makes it tempting to subsume it under the category of what Ryle (*The Concept of Mind*, 1949, pp. 149–54) has called "achievement" concepts—that is, such concepts as finding, winning, arriving, discovering, curing, concealing, scoring, missing, detecting, or getting to know. For discovering and detecting, like noticing, are not activities. They are not something in which we can, either continuously or intermittently, engage; they are not done in a certain manner. We can ask how someone did them— that is, how he managed to do them; but to ask why he did them is to seek reasons for doing what would bring them about, rather than for doing them themselves. Like noticing, they are things we can be quick or slow to reach. Further, noticing is like discovering or detecting in that the reason why we can notice so and so, or fail to notice it—but not "notice erroneously or wrongly"—is that the term itself signifies the correctness of the information acquired. We cannot notice a crack in the cup, if the cup is without blemish.

Here, however, we must distinguish between Rylean achievement-concepts and another type of result-concepts, which I shall call "reception-concepts"; that is, between the idea of achieving something and the idea of receiving something. The category of reception-concepts is one to which not only *noticing* but also, as we shall see, *realizing, becoming conscious of*, and *becoming aware of* must be assigned. It is because both achievement-concepts and reception-concepts signify results and not activities that the logical qualities so far mentioned are shared by such concepts as *discovering* and *detecting* on the one hand, and by *noticing* on the other.

There is, however, an important set of qualities that all achievement-concepts have, but which are quite alien to reception-concepts. An achievement is something one may either try for or resolve to try for, and either manage or fail to obtain; it is something that may be reached by various means and methods or by luck, by one's own efforts or with help. It is the possible culmination of a task. Even when an achievement is not actually prefaced by a task performance, as when it is fortuitous or due to luck, it always makes sense to say that it might have been so prefaced. But noticing, like receiving and unlike achieving, is not something we can spend a long time trying to do, even though it may be at the end of a long and careful examination that we announce "I don't notice anything." Further, what we announce is that we "don't" notice, but that we "can't" discover anything, just as we ask a man whether he "can" find, but whether he "does" notice. We can resolve to, and perhaps manage to score or cure, but not to notice. A failure to discover or conceal something marks an unsuccessful attempt; a failure to notice it marks the non-acquisition of an answer. One can get to know or to score by fair means or foul, and one's method of solving or curing may be direct or devious; but we do not use methods to notice faults, nor are there means for noticing fallacies. We cannot bend our efforts to noticing, nor can others help us to notice. Noticing is not, as achievement is, the objective of a task. We can ask someone how he "would" discover or cure, but not how he "would" notice, although it is as legitimate to ask how he "did" notice as it is to ask how he "did" discover or cure. For the former "how" question asks for the method, but the latter for the opportunity. Although appropriate schooling and practice can put us in a condition to notice what we used to miss, people cannot be taught nor can they learn how to notice, as they can be taught or can learn how to detect. Noticing, unlike solving, is not the exercise of a skill.

An achievement of any kind is something which it makes sense to say that we bring about, even though sometimes it is in fact bestowed on us. Discoveries are made, solutions produced, cures brought about, wins gained, victories secured and successes scored. What we receive, however, comes to us, provided we have been appropriately prepared. We do not produce it or gain it, secure it or bring it off. It is not an investigational triumph. One could not notice a twinge or a stab that one did not feel, nor feel one without noticing it. Yet no one supposes that feeling a twinge of toothache or a stab of pain is an achievement, the successful completion of a task. In noticing a twinge, one receives knowledge of its presence by its catching hold of one's attention. When we notice something, we are struck by it; it makes an impression on us and we receive knowledge of it. What is noticeable is conspicuous or stands out, just as what is interesting attracts attention.

We may be in a position to notice because of our nature or previous training, or because we are on the lookout, or because we are attentive, or because we are interested. Contrariwise, we may fail to notice because we are in one or another of these ways unprepared. The reason why one cannot notice X while all one's attention is on Y is that noticing X implies having our attention caught by it. There are certain features that human beings are commonly trained and adapted to receive. Some things we cannot help noticing; there are others that specific education prepares us for. All of us naturally notice our twinges of toothache. But only a musician could be struck by a similarity between Bach and Irving Berlin; a child would not notice a misquotation from Virgil.

One can be literally struck by something like a brick, without being able to tell *what* struck one; or by something like a feather, without being able to tell *that* one has been struck at all. But to be struck by something in the sense of noticing it is to receive knowledge of it, to be able to tell what it is. Just as we may file away information by making a note of it, so we may acquire knowledge either by making a "mental" note of something or by noticing it. This is why only a bad memory or some other handicap excuses a man from being able to give an account of something he claims to have noticed. It should, however, be emphasized that to assert that "noticing" X entails being able to tell what X is, is not necessarily to assert that a verbal description of X's nature can be given. A person might well be "able to tell" the difference between A and B without being able to say what it is; there are lots of things that animals and infants notice. Nor does noticing X imply that you recognize it as Y. Further, just as A can indicate what B has been giving his attention to, using a description that is unknown to B, it seems that A can also indicate what B has noticed, using a description that is unknown to B. Thus, A may say of B that he noticed or paid particular attention to the new arrival, even though B could not describe in that same way the man he had noticed or paid attention to. B could not, of course, be said to have noticed that there was a new arrival, for, although the presence of the person had caught his attention, his status as a new arrival may not have.

Like other attention-concepts, *notice* is polymorphous. We saw that to pay attention to anything is to make it the object of some of the activities that are appropriate to it. The attentive reader keeps his eyes on the book and his mind on the argument; the attentive audience is looking at, listening to, and thinking of nothing but the play. Similarly, to notice is to be struck or impressed, to have one's attention caught, by some perceptual or intellectual object, or by some activity or feeling about which one thereby receives information. Just as we attend by looking, listening, etc., so seeing (both perceptual and intellectual), hearing, smelling, tasting, touching, and feeling are the forms our noticing takes. We may "notice" or "hear" a false note, "notice" or "see" a flaw in a diamond or a fallacy in an argument. Escaping gas is "noticed" or "smelled," peculiar tastes are noticed when we use our palates. If we notice pains, we feel them. To write "see, hear, *or* notice," instead of "see, hear, or otherwise notice" is to commit the same error as writing "look, listen, *or* attend" for "look, listen, or otherwise attend," or writing "present arms, stand at ease, *or* obey" for "present arms, stand at ease or otherwise obey." The features about which we acquire knowledge when we notice things are not additional to those about which we acquire knowledge when we use our organs of sight, hearing, etc. There is no special organ of noticing, and no "proper object" of the verb "to notice," as there is for any verb of perception.

Since, however, *notice* is a polymorphous concept, we can see or feel things without its being thereby true to say that we "notice" them, just as we can present arms without obeying any order. It is only when what we see or feel is something that stands out and strikes us that we can describe it as something we have noticed—that is, as something that has caught our attention.

We speak of noticing, not the whole valley spread out, but the houses in the foreground; not the entire agenda, but a single item on it. We may notice the man's clothes instead of the general background, his tie rather than the clothes, the design on the tie rather than the tie. It is by attending to the diamond that we notice the fault, by attending to the piece of music that we notice the false note. Further, "notice," unlike "see," cannot be used to signify the basic visual capacity that only the blind lack, nor the way in which we keep something in sight for a few minutes. Nor does "notice," like "see," signify an achievement, or a piece of detection. This is why any talk of ability or skill, of teaching or learning, of effort or trial, is altogether out of place. Similarly, we may feel various mild sensations all over our body that we would not say we notice, because they do not normally stand out and attract our attention, or make themselves known to us. Other things being equal, the more intense a sensation becomes, the more it stands out or becomes noticeable. We are not said to "notice," as we are said to "feel," thrills or glows, perhaps because these are not something we are struck by, as by a stab of pain, but something spread out and unlocalized, something continuous that grips us and holds us; we can notice, however, that we feel a thrill or a glow, and we can also become and remain aware or conscious of these sensations. Words like "stab," "twinge," "throb," "pang," and sometimes "pain" and "itch," refer to something in our experience that stands out from the surroundings and which, therefore, we notice. If we had a group of bodily sensations all equally intense, as we might have a group of visual sensations all equally dazzling, there would be no reason why we should notice one rather than another. Only when a sensation is felt as such—different from or standing out from the others—has it made itself known to us by catching our attention; only then have we noticed it.

The fact that what we notice stands out from other things is reflected in the grammar of the word "notice." We speak of noticing the color *of* a tie, the tie *on* the table, and the table *in* the room; we notice the chimes *of* the clock, the twinge *in* the tooth, and the throb *of* the pain. This same fact is emphasized in the work of psychologists by their distinction between the "figure" and the "ground" in perception. Something can be seen as such, only if it seems to stand out from its background.

Consciousness

To become conscious of something and to remain conscious of it is to have one's attention caught and held by it, to have it before one's mind, in perception, feeling, or thought. We talk, perhaps in jargon, about the threshold, the margin, the fringe and the center of consciousness, as well as about the possibility of something's entering into or going out of consciousness. We saw that one of Freud's reasons for postulating "the Unconscious" was the fact that lots of things that we know are not at the moment actually being thought of or recalled. They must, therefore, he thought, exist somewhere outside our consciousness, namely in the Unconscious or the Pre-conscious. Another similar reason was the fact that we are influenced by fears and hopes, desires and needs, thoughts and wishes, which we do not always, and sometimes cannot, openly entertain or occupy ourselves with, and of whose existence we may thus be unaware.

Being conscious or unconscious *of* so and so is not the same as simply being conscious or unconscious. If there is anything of which a man is conscious, it follows that he is conscious; to lose consciousness is to cease to be conscious of *anything*. But to be conscious, as we all are when we are not asleep or drugged, etc., is not incompatible with our being unconscious of X or Y. To act unconsciously, therefore, is not to act while unconscious.

"Conscious of" and "conscious that" are sometimes used dispositionally—that is, to indicate that there is a tendency on specific occasions to be conscious of or conscious that. A man is said to be "class-conscious," "safety-conscious," or "cost-conscious," if he tends to be conscious of his social background, of possible dangers, or of the price of things. Commonly, however, the terms "conscious of" and "conscious that" are used to report a present experience. There is some particular object of which one is conscious. Nor do we remain conscious, as we can remain aware, of what no longer holds our attention.

Further, since to become conscious of something at any one moment is the beginning of both being and remaining conscious of it, what we become and are conscious of, unlike what we notice, must be something continuous. We can notice, but not become or be conscious of, a flash of light or a stab of pain, while we become conscious of, rather than notice, a feeling of misery or of satisfaction. What we become conscious of, unlike what we notice, must also be something that existed before we became conscious of it.

What we are at any moment conscious of is often something present, which occupies us in perception, feeling, or thought. We may be conscious of a noise, a pain in the back, the hostility of the audience, or the fact that the furniture has been rearranged. Or we may be conscious of what we are now doing, such as assuming so and so or adhering to such and such a rule. Sometimes, what one is conscious of is some enduring characteristic, such as the defects of one's intellect or the advantages of someone's plan. We can, however, now be conscious of something that happened in the past, such as an honor recently received or the circumstances of one's birth, if these things are occupying our present thoughts.

In consciousness of a perceptual object, such as a sound or a man, our attention is held by what we perceive. Being conscious of it is not an alternative to our continuing to see or to hear it, nor does it imply some organ that is additional to eyes and ears, nor does it discover properties other than the visible or the audible. Perception of something, however, is not consciousness of it, any more than it is noticing it. Only those things that we realize we see are things we are conscious of; a man who sees a bush and thinks it is a rabbit is not conscious of the bush. Further, we are not conscious of something we see unless it impresses itself on us—that is, unless it catches and *holds* our attention. We do not say that we are conscious of things in our general field of vision or smell, nor of things that do not stand out from others or that are only momentarily seen or heard.

To be conscious of what we are doing, in the sense of doing it consciously, is to know what we are doing because it is what we are currently occupied with; it is what is engaging our attention as the intentional move we are currently making.

Most things of which we are conscious are things that we can be said, in one sense or another, to "feel," or which make themselves felt. Thus we may be acutely, deeply, or faintly conscious of sinking feelings in the stomach, of slight misgivings about a plan, of our own ignorance or inadequacy, of the friendliness of the crowd, or of the spectators' eyes on us. We may be agreeably or uncomfortably, pleasantly or painfully, conscious of so and so. The man who is conscious that the room has been rearranged feels, and rightly so, that it has; he feels a sort of strangeness that is warranted by the situation. To be class-conscious is to feel acutely about matters of social class and class relations.

Consciousness involves both attention and knowledge; to be conscious of something is both to have it in mind—even to feel it—and to be right in so feeling. What we are conscious of is there or is so, and we know it to be there or to be so. A person could not be conscious of his own weakness of will, however much he might feel that he was unreliable, if in fact his character was strong. The feeling that something has been changed differs from the consciousness that it has, in that the former is open to correction, while the latter is not. Just as noticing our momentary feelings implies both feeling them and knowing them to be momentarily there, so being conscious of our continuous feelings implies both feeling them and knowing them to be continuously there. Since we do not feel other people's feelings, however intense they may be, to notice or to be conscious of their feelings—whether of misery, embarrassment, or dislike—is not to feel these as they feel them, but to feel correctly that they are thus affected. I can be, in different ways, conscious of my own or another's misery, but only in my own case can I be conscious of a pricking sensation behind the eyeballs.

We may feel a twinge and not know that we feel jealous, or we may feel a prick and not know that it is a nail. Yet we cannot feel a twinge and not know what we feel, nor feel inclined to do something and not know what it is we feel inclined to do. Now those feelings that we cannot fail to know we have, like those feelings of whose existence we are not in fact ignorant, are necessarily feelings of which we are conscious; to be conscious of them is to feel them and to know what it is that we feel. That is why Locke held that "To be happy or miserable without being conscious of it seems to me utterly inconsistent and impossible."

Since feelings are not the sorts of things one perceives, to be conscious of them is not to perceive them, nor, *a fortiori*, to "introspect" them, as many traditional philosophers have pointed out. A person cannot fail to be conscious of—that is, to feel—his angry feelings at their height; but, as Hume and Reid observed, there is an incongruity in expecting a cool and attentive examination of them at such a time. Reid also emphasized that consciousness is "common to all men at all times" whereas "the habit of reflection is . . . not to be attained without much pains and practice." Having feelings, unlike introspection and retrospection, is not something we could acquire a habit of, or be trained in.

Because "consciousness of" something signifies the way in which the knowledge of it holds our attention, and not the mere acquisition or possession of the knowledge, the concept of *consciousness* differs in many respects from that of *knowledge*. We can qualify the completeness of our con-

sciousness, but not of our knowledge, as "clear" or "full,"
while our knowledge, but not our consciousness, may be
characterized as "thorough," "intimate," or "detailed."
More importantly, we do not become conscious, as we may
come to know, from any sources, whether direct or authori-
tative, or by any methods, such as experiments, reasoning,
or observation, or as a result of some evidence.

The difference between the knowledge we have by way
of observation, reasoning, etc., and the knowledge we have
through our being conscious of something, throws light on
three problems that have recently been puzzling philosophers. First, the positions of our limbs, our spasms and our
reflex reactions are all things of which we are conscious.
Secondly, if someone says that he is in pain, it seems
absurd to ask him how he knows this or whether he has
any doubt about it. The ideas of detection, evidence, and
criteria are quite out of place in such a case. Some philosophers who have noted this have concluded, wrongly, that
an utterance such as "I feel an itch" can be only an
avowal of one's feeling, and not a report on its existence,
while others have doubted the meaningfulness of the expression "I know I'm in pain." The truth is that knowledge
of our continuous sensations is consciousness of them, that
is, indeed, a kind of knowledge to which means, methods,
and evidence are irrelevant. Thirdly, the knowledge I have
of what I am intentionally doing does not come to me by
way of examination of or reflection upon what I am doing.
That is how we discover the intentions of others. What I
do intentionally, I know I am doing, because it is what I
am occupied in bringing about; it is what currently holds
my attention. What I do intentionally, therefore, I do consciously.

When we consciously assume something we also knowingly act in certain ways, such as saying so and so, which
we know amounts to such an assumption. But our knowledge that saying so and so amounts to that assumption is
not the result of any examination of what we say; it has
its origin in the fact that the very utterance of the remark
is dictated by the assumption. It is because we are know-

ingly assuming such and such that we make the remark
we do; it is not that, as the result of making this remark,
we can properly be said to have knowingly assumed such
and such. A man might realize with surprise that he was
doing so and so, but surprise would be impossible for him
if he were consciously doing it. The metaphors of "flashing" and "dawning," which are appropriate to realization
and discovery, are out of place in our knowledge of what
we are doing intentionally.

There are further differences between *consciousness* and
knowledge. We can know, yet not be conscious of, a language or a game. To be conscious of our skill in that language or game is not merely to know that we possess it,
but to be impressed by our possession of it. To be conscious of a person, as either present or absent, is not to be
acquainted with him, but to have a continuous awareness
of him. We can know someone we are not at present conscious of; we can be conscious of someone whom we do
not know. The store of information that most of us collect
and file away during our lives forms part of what we know,
but not of what we are conscious of. A historian is not
necessarily conscious of the date of the battle of Austerlitz,
although a country may be conscious of its history. Nor is
an astronomer necessarily conscious of the distance of
Alpha Centauri, although Kant was often conscious of the
majesty of the stars.

We need not always or ever be conscious of what we
know. In our consciousness of something external—such as
a movement in the corner or the friendliness of the audience—the knowledge that it is there occupies our mind
and influences our behavior; its presence makes itself felt.
We say that people are conscious of the TV camera that
is focused on them, when they cannot behave naturally
because the knowledge that they are being filmed holds
some of their attention, and thus affects their behavior.
People who are conscious of their race, color, profession, or
status cannot keep these out of their thinking and their
overt behavior.

Care

"Care" sometimes means worry or anxiety: to be full of care is to be worried; to be carefree is to have no worries.

To be free from care is not the same, however, as not caring. Whatever the Cynics and Stoics may have thought, indifference is an effective, yet not the only, insurance against anxiety. The saint who does not care about the world's opinion is inclined not to pay any attention to it. The carefree child may or may not give his attention to something; when he does, he is not worried by it.

Serenity, or freedom from care, and indifference, or not caring, are distinct not only from each other and from inattention, but also from carelessness. A careful person is someone who takes care; he need not be either worried or interested. To be too worried, or full of care, may in fact render a person incapable of taking proper care, or even of being careful. Sometimes, indeed, we do not bother because we cannot be bothered, and sometimes we take care because we do care; but these are not always so. The objects of anxiety and indifference, like those of attention and interest, are legion; but we can take care only of what is under our own control. Whether or not we care what we say about others and what they say about us, we can exercise care only in what we say about them.

This distinction between the care of the careful and the care of the not indifferent enables us to explain two well-known conflicts in jurisprudence. The first is about the nature of *negligence*—that is, culpable carelessness. Subjectivists such as John Salmond defined "negligence" as the act of a man who does not care, while Objectivists such as Frederick Pollock defined it as conduct that consists in a failure to take precautions against harm. It is clear, however, that the Subjectivists have assimilated the concept of carelessness to that of indifference—that is, to not caring.

The second conflict is about the nature of *recklessness*. The Subjectivists define "recklessness" as not caring

whether the realized risks of one's actions take place or
not, while the Objectivists define it as not taking care to
see that the realized risks of one's actions do not take place.
Consequently, the Objectivists affirm and the Subjectivists
deny that recklessness is a form or degree of negligence—
if negligence is objective. Judicial decisions can be found
in favor of either side. On the nature of recklessness, however, it is the Subjectivists who are in accordance with
ordinary use. For recklessness is a form of indifference—
namely, an indifference to the realized risks of one's action
—so great that one is not deterred from going on with the
action. We can feel reckless, but not negligent; be in a
reckless, but not a negligent mood; act in a spirit of recklessness, but not of negligence. We can be perfectly or
absolutely reckless—that is, without any concern at all; but
we can be only extremely or grossly negligent—that is,
with the greatest carelessness. Recklessness may sometimes
explain our negligence; it is not ever a form of it.

Having distinguished the care of the careful both from
the care of the not indifferent and from the care of the
anxious, we should also remember that, in characterizing a
man or his actions as "careful," we may mean that he
exercised care either *when* doing what he did or *by* doing
what he did. As we saw in the first section of this chapter,
attention-concepts sometimes have this double role: that
of describing the manner in which someone acts, and that
of explaining his commissions and omissions. In both roles,
care is a polymorphous concept, so that the exercise of care
necessarily takes the form of a specific deed; but only in
its explanatory role does the concept *care* go to form a
"mongrel-categorical" statement. The man who carefully
keeps to the left of the road does so because he is taking
care; but the man who drives carefully does not do so
because he is taking care.

What exactly do we mean when we say of someone that
he takes care when doing something? Although a man
could no more do something with care while his attention
was not on it, than he could show an interest in something without paying attention to it, the way in which

attention is a sign of care is quite different from the way in which it is a sign of interest. The man who is taking an interest in his driving is giving his attention to it as the following of an inclination to attend, whereas the man who is taking care when he is driving is paying attention to certain features that are appropriate to successful driving.

Not all attention, however, is a sign of care, any more than it is a sign of interest. This is particularly obvious in the spectator-type of attention. The viewer whose attention is glued to his television set is not necessarily exercising any care; nor is the morbid introspectionist. Even when we are doing something with attention, we need not be doing it with care. To say that a child is absorbed in his drawing, or an adult in his gardening, is neither to say nor to deny anything about the care or lack of care exhibited. To call one's lover "attentive" is a compliment; to call him "careful" might be an insult. To train a man to be attentive is not to train him to be careful.

In order to carry on any task smoothly and successfully, there are certain things one must do and certain others one has to avoid doing, or prevent from happening. Every task has its peculiar and appropriate mistakes, errors, accidents, dangers, and pitfalls. Apart from skill and knowledge, these can be avoided only by giving active and practical attention to them and to insurances against them. Care is the giving of this attention to such risks and to the insurances against them. The person who exercises care in doing something has to be careful to do so and so and also careful not to do such and such.

Because *care*, like other *attention* concepts, is polymorphous, the specific form that it takes varies from task to task. We could not know what a person was specifically doing merely from being told that he was taking care, or what characterized his behavior merely from the description that he was a careful man, any more than we could know what a person who was repeating himself must be specifically doing. Conversely, the behavior that in certain circumstances or in a certain class of person would be properly described as "careful" might not deserve this description in different circumstances, or from a person of a different position. The careful speaker watches his choice of words; the careful proofreader is on the look-out for misprints. We lift things carefully, tenderly, and gently, or we search carefully and methodically; our dress is careless and untidy, our essay careless and slipshod.

There is, it is clear, a note of appraisal in the notion of *care*. The careless man is considered not to have done what he ought to have done. This note of appraisal is partly due to the social fact that we approve of actions that do not injure others and disapprove of those that do. Hence, also, the great interest that the law has in care and negligence. Insofar as care has this evaluative element, it shares with such a notion as *good* the combination of a stable meaning with a discussible set of standards. It is a matter for discussion what are to count in different sorts of cases as the things to which attention ought to be given, and what amount of attention ought to be given to them. These are questions that the law considers under "standard of care." A judge, for instance, knows perfectly well that "ordinary care" means the same thing, whether he is considering the conduct of an engine-driver or of a manufacturer of proprietary drugs; what he has to decide is what is to count as such care in relationship to each.

Interest

Interest is something we have, show, or feel. We can "be interested" in—that is, have an interest in—an object without at a given moment showing or feeling that interest. To say of someone that he is too interested in the faults of men to see their virtues is to comment on his general character, not on present performance. But to "be interested" can also mean that one is now showing or feeling an interest. Thus, to speak of someone as being too interested in his book to hear the doorbell is to refer to a specific episode. To characterize someone as "being interested in," or "having an interest in" something, is to say that he is

prone to feel and to show an interest in it. His dispositional interest is manifested by his occurrent interest. Since
we can have a dispositional interest that is not at the moment active, however, interest cannot, as some psychologists have thought, be equated with attention. Nor will the
equation of interest with attention hold for either the
actual display or the present feeling of interest. A man who
is at this moment showing an interest in something must
be paying attention to it; he can also pay attention, however, without showing, or even having, any interest. To
feel at a particular moment interested in something is to
feel attracted to it, to feel inclined to give it attention. But
I can also pay attention at a particular moment without
feeling any inclination to do so.

Psychologists have, more commonly, analyzed interest as
attention plus feeling. This is correct, though we do need
to make clear in what sense we "feel" interested in anything. Someone who is interested in what he is doing does
not necessarily feel any sensations, faint or acute, steady or
intermittent, localizable or general. Such sensations might,
in fact, distract him from the object of his interest.

Interest is not a mood, like cheerfulness or gloominess;
it has a definite object. Nor does it color one's actions and
feelings, as a mood does. An apparent objection is that
boredom, the opposite of interest, can be a mood. The
answer is that "bored" is used to cover both a mood—a
general inability to feel interested in anything—and also a
specific inability to feel interested in a specific topic. A
bored person is, for the moment, without an interest in
anything, just as a confident person is free from doubt and
a fit person is free from illness. Hence, one may be "absolutely," "completely," or "perfectly" bored, but "acutely,"
"intensely," or "deeply" interested.

Feeling interested is, further, not an emotional or
stirred-up state, such as feeling excited or thrilled, agitated
or surprised. You cannot be "beside yourself" or "speech-
less" with interest; nor does increasing interest disturb
your concentration, as mounting excitement or anxiety
may.

To feel interested in anything is to feel attracted to it, to feel inclined to give attention to it. Naturally, this also involves feeling disinclined to attend to other things, and feeling vexed, unhappy, and uncomfortable, when prevented from giving attention to this one. Thus, a man who feels an interest in what is happening across the road will feel inclined to give his attention to it; if there is nothing to stop him, he will in fact be prone to do so. Further, a man who feels inclined to do something, such as paying attention, when he is prevented from doing so, will have a strong feeling of frustration. A man who is actually doing what he feels inclined to do is free from any feeling of frustration; yet it is still true of him that he feels like doing, and perhaps wants to do, what in fact he is doing.

When interest passes over into *fascination*, our inclination to attend is not so much evidence of a desire to do so as of an inability not to do so. We attend, not because we want to, but because we cannot help it. To be fascinated by a snake is to be unable to take your eyes off it; the man who is fascinated by a woman cannot stop thinking about her.

Attention may be demanded; interest has to be aroused. "Conscientious," "deliberate," "willing," "half-hearted," "reluctant," and "unwilling" are appropriate to attention, but not to interest, since interest already contains the idea of being attracted and of paying attention because you feel inclined that way. It is conceptually different, and also more flattering, to say that you read someone's book with deep interest than to say that you read it with close attention. It is unfair to blame someone for not showing any interest, but not unfair to blame him for lack of attention. Trying to get interested in something is somewhat like trying to feel sorry for someone; neither is a matter of trying to *do*. This is why we often say that someone might at least look interested or pretend to be interested, just as we say that he might look sorry or pretend to feel sorry. Having or showing an interest is not something we can decide, resolve, or refuse to do, as we can decide, resolve, or refuse to pay attention. Being interested or uninterested is something we cannot here and now help.

Interest, like attention, is polymorphous. Just as "attending" does not signify one particular activity, so "interest" does not signify an inclination to engage in one particular activity. Interest is an inclination to engage in some one or more perceptual, intellectual, or practical activities that are appropriate to the particular object of interest.

Interest, in its dispositional use, can provide an explanation for engaging in any activity and, therefore, for paying attention. An interest in archaeology may explain why someone pays attention to archaeological matters by reading books, attending lectures, and joining in conversations on the subject. We often attend to something for its own sake—that is, because we are interested in it; but the reason why we attend may also be that we are interested in finding out or discovering something. "Curiosity" is the name of this sort of interest. Interest may also provide an indirect explanation of our noticing things, since it is attention that enables us to notice. The sort of explanation that interest provides for paying attention to something or for engaging in any activity is similar to that which jealousy provides for certain kinds of behavior, and to that which brittleness provides for breakages. When you wish to attract someone's attention, you try to provide the sort of thing that is likely to do this. One such thing is something in which that person is interested. Advertisers' billboard posters show pictures of pretty girls because "sex-interested" males will, by definition, look at them. We are all probably familiar with the anecdotes of the psychology textbooks, the point of which is that people of different interests, when they are placed in the same situation, pay attention to and often notice quite different features. On their communal walk, the geologist notices the rock formation; the botanist, the plant life; the painter, features of the landscape; the philosopher fails to notice anything at all. The point illustrated is not a factual discovery about

human behavior, not something for which we need experimental evidence; it is a logical truth about the relation
of the notions of *attention* and *notice* to that of *interest*.
The important questions of empirical psychology, on the
other hand, are concerned with the reasons why people
have the interests they do have and lack those that they
do not have.

When what we do, including the paying of attention to
something, is explained, not by a continuing interest that
we have, but by an interest we are here and now showing
or feeling, the explanation is of a different kind. Since to
feel interested is to feel inclined to pay attention, then to
pay attention to something because we feel interested in
it is to do what we feel inclined to do.

It follows from this relation of *interest* to *attention* that
the statement "He showed an interest in so and so" is a
Rylean "mongrel-categorical," relative to the statement "He
paid attention to so and so." A reporter might say of a
distinguished visitor at an exhibition either that he paid
particular attention to the toy stand or that he showed a
particular interest in it. The description in terms of interest
gives an explanatory-cum-predictive account of the same
event as the description in terms of attention.

We can, however, distinguish between saying of someone that he is doing what he does "with" interest and saying that he is doing it "from," "for," or "out of" interest.
"With interest" tells us that what he is doing arouses and
retains his interest; "from interest" gives an explanation for
his doing it. Hence, words such as "purely," "solely," and
"merely," which emphasize the uniqueness of an explanation, can qualify "from interest," but not "with interest,"
whereas terms of degree, such as "little," "much," "intense," and "increasing" can qualify "with interest," but
not "from interest."

CHAPTER 4

Thought

The characteristic that is traditionally associated with the mind is thought. It is by his power of thought that man has often been differentiated from the animals, or one man rated above his fellows. The history of the human race comprises the history of action and the history of thought. Descartes divided the universe into extended things and thinking things; Marx included among workers those by hand and those by brain.

Since both psychologists and philosophers are interested in answering the question "What is thought?," it is important to distinguish clearly between an examination of the meaning of "thought," and an examination of the features of thought. In the former, we are analyzing a concept; in the latter, a phenomenon. The former is philosophy; the latter, psychology. The question of whether "thought" refers to a power, an activity, or an attainment, is philosophical; the question of whether, in thinking, the muscles of the larynx are moved is psychological. Philosophical and psychological inquiries are sometimes assimilated because of a failure to distinguish between an examination of what is meant by—that is, the meaning of—a word, and an examination of what is meant by—that is, the object or situation referred to by—a word.

Yet the inquiries of the philosophy of thought are germane to its psychology. For instance, if a philosophical

analysis were to show that what is being studied in studying the judgments we make are not acts of thought, but
results of thought, that would explain why the psychologist
Marbe's attempts to find an act of judgment met with
failure. If a philosophical analysis were to show that
"thinking" does not designate a specific activity, but indicates a relationship between a specific activity and its circumstances, that would explain why the Wurzburg School's
direct introspection of pieces of thinking did not reveal the
nature of thinking. The fact, discovered in 1906 by the
psychologists Watt and Messer, that a person's judgment
that X is Y is different from his mere association of the
ideas of X and Y—because in a judgment there is a question or task in the offing—is a philosophical rather than a
psychological fact. The non-psychological nature of the
discovery is even clearer for those everyday judgments in
which the subject is not aware of any question at the
moment of making the judgment.

The two most striking features of the concept of *thought*
are the variety of separate uses of the word "think"—that
is, the ambiguity of "think"—and the polymorphous character of each of these uses.

The Ambiguity of "Think"

English, unlike some other languages, uses the one word
"think" and its variants to cover several aspects of the
workings of our intellect. "Think" is used of our activity
when we are musing, puzzling or paying attention, of our
success in getting hold of or being struck by a solution,
and of our power to find one; it denotes our possession of
such a solution, or of some other opinion or concept, as
well as the intended application of our words.

AS SIGNIFYING AN ACTIVITY

To think may be to engage in some activity. We can be
thinking continuously or intermittently, for a moment or all
morning, with or without interruption, silently or out loud.

What I am thinking about holds my non-perceptual attention, just as what I am looking at or listening to holds my visual or aural attention. But whereas I cannot look at or listen to what is not there, I can think about the non-existent as easily as I can about the existent.

Such an activity may be of several kinds.

1. I am thinking when I (idly or seriously) review something from the past, or dwell in anticipation on something in the future, or daydream about possibilities. Sometimes I cannot help thinking about a thing, perhaps because it was a nasty accident, or because it is a forthcoming test. It captures and holds my attention. I may be asked to think about a proposal, I may keep on thinking about it, or I may soon cease to think about it. Such thinking may be pleasant, frightening, compulsive or distracting, but there is no question of its being efficient, unmethodical, purposeful or successful. I am occupied, but not puzzlingly occupied. To be always thinking of someone is to be unable to forget him; gradually to forget him is to think of him less and less.

2. I am thinking what I am doing when my attention is given to my deed or to some aspect of it. The more difficult, delicate or unusual my task, the more I may have to think what I am doing. For example, I have to think what I am doing when I am cleaning an Old Master, but not when I am cleaning a window. To neglect some aspect of my deed is to be guilty of lack of thought—to be absent-minded, careless, tactless, or thoughtless. A thoughtless person is not someone who never puzzles over anything; he is someone who pays no attention to the effects of his actions on others. I may partly or particularly, carefully or anxiously, think what I am doing, but I cannot systematically, efficiently, or unsuccessfully think what I am doing. I can be advised to think before I act, just as I can be warned to look before I leap.

3. I may be thinking about something because I have a problem to solve. How shall I earn enough money for a holiday? Where shall I go if I get the money? I am occupied by the problem; I am trying to get hold of, to think

of, an answer. This answer may be something I am trying to remember, to discover, or to create. It may be a truth about the world, a decision about what to do, a plan of campaign, a new method, or a new project. Such solution-seeking thinking may be strenuous, time-consuming, successful, or unsuccessful. It may come up to or fall short of certain standards of rigor, care, and reasonableness. It may stick to the point and proceed methodically, or it may be irrelevant and wandering. It may be brilliant or pedestrian. It may employ various means and methods— these are of interest to psychologists—in reaching its objective. It may use words or images, musical notes or mathematical symbols, paints or plasticine, although it does not use a peculiar (material or immaterial) organ. Using your brains, your wits, or your intelligence is not analogous to using your eyes, your hands, or your feet. To use your hands without your wits is not to neglect one organ; it is to use your hands unintelligently. We do not think with our mind, or with our brain, in the same way as we see with our eyes or hear with our ears. "Use your head" may be literal advice to the panting wrestler; it is only metaphorical advice to the stupid schoolboy. I can do this kind of thinking out loud or in my head, on my own or in co-operation with others. Not only can I carry it on without any success, I may be unable, through panic or fatigue, even to get down to doing it at all.

AS SIGNIFYING A RESULT

1. To think may not be to engage in any activity, but to get hold of or to receive a particular thought at a particular time. In other words, I may either manage or happen to think of something. What I think of may be something I sought or something that came unsought; I may have hit on it or it may just have occurred to me. If it is something I sought, I may have found it immediately or only after some effort. Upon being asked, I can without effort think of my wife's maiden name, although I have to think hard to recall the name of my first Latin teacher. At other

times both names may come to me unsought, or something else may make me think of them. To hit upon or be struck by a thought is to think of it; to search for it is to be thinking. However little or long I may spend thinking before I think of it, to think of it does not itself take time. However greatly method and efficiency in my thinking may help me to think of something, I do not think of it methodically or efficiently. A failure to think of what I am trying to think of is not a failure to think; nor is success in thinking of it a bit of thinking. Finding a solution is not a piece of solution-seeking. Problem solving is not a species of trying to solve a problem. To ask why I am thinking about something is to ask for a reason; to ask why I thought of it is to ask for a cause, for what made me think of it. What I think of, whether out of the blue or during a search for an answer to a problem, catches my attention. It may or may not continue to hold it—that is, I may or may not go on thinking about it.

What I think of I may or may not think of as being so and so. I can think not merely of X and of Y but that X is related to Y. While addressing Christmas cards, I may be reminded of your last year's card, or struck by the fact that your card was exactly like the one I am now sending you. But to think of X and of Y is not necessarily to think that X is related to Y: I can be reminded of your card without thinking that it was like mine. To tell the psychiatrist what comes to one's mind when he says "beer" or "bed" is not to express an opinion; the mere association of ideas is not a judgment. What distinguishes a judgment from such simple association is not the presence of some additional experienced element, but the fact that the association of ideas expresses the answer to an explicit or implicit question. It was this absence of any additional experienced element in the judgment that puzzled early psychologists in their attempts to distinguish judgment from association. The thought *of* something, unlike the thought *that* something, is neither correct nor incorrect, reasonable or unreasonable, brilliant or commonplace.

If, when I think of something, I think of it as being so

and so, it may be something I am trying to remember, or discover, or create. I may, for instance, have been trying to think where I last saw you, or how you have changed, or in what way I can make you comfortable. If my thought is correct, then I have remembered or discovered or created what I think I have. Depending on the position that it occupies in my thinking, my thinking that so and so may, on different occasions, constitute reaching a conclusion, committing a fallacy, seeing an objection, etc.

Unsought thoughts result neither from trying, nor from the easy exercise of a skill. They may also be merely the thought of something, as when I am reminded of a friend; or a thought that something is so, as when I suddenly think that I have forgotten my umbrella. If the unsought thought that X is Y is correct, it may be that I noticed, or became aware of, or realized, or recognized, that X is Y. When this observation is brilliant and inexplicable, it may be called an inspiration or intuition.

What I come to think to be so—whether the thought be attained gradually or like lightning, as a result of effort, effortlessly or unsought, and whether, if it is correct, it be the product of memory, detection, creation, or realization—may be that something is true or funny, stupid or unfair, tasteless or foul, probable, inevitable, or impossible. My coming to think it may be expressed in an exclamatory sentence, in a laugh of appreciation, a look of horror, or a cry of protest, or in an anticipatory or evasive movement.

2. The ability, when we are confronted with a problem, to think of the right answer, or of a step toward the right answer, is our power of thought—whether of memory, discovery, or creation. The strength of this power may depend partly upon our innate constitution, partly on practice and learning, and partly on using the appropriate methods. Good habits of thought can be inculcated just as can good habits of behavior. It is this power of thought that is tested by memory tests, intelligence tests, and games of skill, and which distinguishes the good memory from the bad, the able thinker from the poor, and the quick-witted from the slow. I may confess shamefacedly, after some move in a

problem has been pointed out to me, that I had never thought of that. It is the same power that is exercised both in our hard-won and in our effortless successes in producing the right answers or in behaving appropriately. I can think easily of a dozen English nouns, not so easily of a dozen Italian nouns, and, only after much trying, of a dozen Spanish nouns. This power of thought is exercised when we spot a mistake or formulate an objection. It is also exercised in the continuous following of an argument. It may be seen both in our arrival at a solution and in our hitting upon factors that bring us nearer the solution. As a skill in accomplishing things, it has canons of success and failure, as well as of effective and ineffective methods. It has its experts and its novices, its teachers and its pupils. The successes it scores can be contrasted with those that are due to luck.

This ability to think of things, to reach conclusions, to solve problems, must not be confused, however, either with the ability to pay attention to the problem, or with the ability to attempt to solve it. Nor is the thinking that is the attempt to think of a solution an exercise of the capacity to think of the solution. There is a difference between thinking and good, intelligent, thinking. Many psychologists have tended to run together, under the general heading of "problem-solving," both the act of thinking, which constitutes an attempt to solve a problem, and the successful thinking of a solution. They have, further, tended to examine thinking only in this problem-solving form, as Bruner and Bartlett have done. What is mainly of interest to psychologists is the methods employed, by animals or humans, in a piece of thinking that is aimed at the thinking of a solution. Thorndike asked whether thinkers use trial and error in their problem-solving, while Kohler asked whether they use insight. Bruner has suggested that we discover concepts by focusing or scanning strategies. Bartlett examined the ways in which we use supplied information in order to reach our goal. His recent definition of thinking as a "high-level skill" admittedly neglects the other varieties of thinking in favor of our ability, and the exercise of this ability, to solve problems, or "to get some-where." But neither puzzling over a problem nor day-dreaming about future success is a skill. There are no expert puzzlers, nor are there novice daydreamers.

AS SIGNIFYING THE POSSESSION OF AN OPINION

1. "To think" may signify neither the activity of thinking, nor the achievement or reception of a thought, but the possession of a thought. We ask, in this sense, not what a man is thinking about, nor what he thought of, but what he thinks. I may long have had and still have the thought that so and so is such and such, or the thought of doing so and so, although I am not at the moment engaged in thinking about it, nor have I just now come to think of it. I began to think when I first tried to exercise my mind, but I began to think that so and so was the case only when the evidence led me to this view, or when I accepted it from someone. The signs that dogs think are signs of mental activity, whereas the signs that the Government thinks that war is inevitable are signs that it holds this opinion. The man who cannot help thinking about the next election is constantly preoccupied with a question, but the man who cannot help thinking that Government policy is wrong is a man who feels forced to adopt a certain answer.

To think that so and so is such and such is not to do anything; it is to be liable to, or to tend to do something —e.g. to assert that so and so is such and such, or to behave in ways that would be appropriate, if so and so were such and such. To think that Homer wrote the Iliad is not tiring, time-consuming, or subject to interruption, nor is it crowned with either success or failure. To think it may, on the other hand, be right or foolish, fashionable or dangerous; it may be due to one's own or another's thinking. To think that so and so will happen just because we would like it to happen is to indulge in wishful thinking. The possession of an opinion that I am not now dwelling on, like the realization or awareness of a truth that does not at the moment hold my attention, is as common and unparadoxical as the possession of knowledge that I am not currently recalling. Indeed, if the thought I possess is correct, and reasonably held, then my holding it may constitute awareness, realization, or some other kind of knowledge.

2. If you ask for someone's thoughts on a particular topic —that is, what he thinks; if you discover them, either from what he says or from what he does; if you assess them as false, pernicious, foolish, or reasonable, then what you are asking for, discovering, or assessing, is the opinions that he currently holds on that topic. These thoughts, as contrasted with the having of them or the reaching of them, can be examined, related, and criticized, according to the canons of logic and truth. The qualification of a remark by the addition of the words "I think," or "Aristotle thought," is not the addition of a gratuitous reference to my thought processes or to those of Aristotle, but an indication of the standing of the remark as the opinion of myself or Aristotle.

Depending on how I arrived at my opinion, and the logical place it has in relation to my evidence and my conclusions, the thought that so and so is the case may be called an assumption, a supposition, a conclusion, a judgment, an assessment, etc. These and similar words describe my thought, not in terms of its content, but in terms of its logical relations to other thoughts.

AS SIGNIFYING THE POSSESSION OF A CONCEPT

Related to the use of "think" to signify the possession of an opinion is its use to mark the possession of a concept. To possess the concept of *time* is to think of things as being before or after one another, as present, past, or future, as enduring or momentary, etc. To use this concept is to think of a particular example as related in one of these ways. Similarly, to possess the concept of *vermilion* is to be able and liable to think of things as being alike in regard to a particular shade of red; to do this is to classify and distinguish things into "vermilion" and "not vermilion."

Our concepts are the ways we think. This is revealed in the way we act, and are ready to act, toward things: in whether we group them together or distinguish them from one another, in whether we expect from them these or those consequences, etc.

AS SIGNIFYING WHAT IS MEANT

To ask what I am thinking of may be to ask what is intended to be covered, or what is meant, by what I said. It is how I would take what I said. I may, for instance, explain that in speaking a moment ago of the burdens of office, I was thinking particularly of the responsibility for making decisions. This is not the same thing as saying that, as I spoke those words, the thought of the responsibility occurred to me, or that I was for a few moments dwelling on it, or distracted by it. The phrase "What I was thinking of, when I said that" refers to the time of speaking, but not to an experience at that time, whereas the phrase "What I thought of, when I said that" refers both to the time of speaking and, in a way to be explained below, to an experience at that time. What I was thinking of by certain words is shown not by what occurred to me, but by how I would react to subsequent events, by what consequences I am prepared or unprepared for. What I was thinking of is what I meant, what I was referring to. If my words are ambiguous, then what I meant may be one or another among the meanings of the words, one among the varied ways in which they could be taken. For example, it is because I was thinking about the passage of time, and not about measuring the speed of insects, when I said, "Time flies; we cannot," that I was disconcerted by your completion of my thought, "They go too fast." To say of something that I never thought of it like that, that I did not take it that way, is to confess that certain consequences of it took me by surprise.

Furthermore, if what I was referring to when I said "London" can also be correctly described in another way —e.g., as the capital of England—then it follows that, whether I realize it or not, I was referring to the capital of England. And, since it is true that I was referring to this, it is also true, in one sense, that I was thinking of this, had this in mind, meant this. Hence, to ask someone whether, when he said "X," he was thinking of "Y," is to try to discover what is being referred to by "X"; it is not to try to discover whether there was a particular description under which it occurred to him. Phrases like "thinking of" and "having in mind" may misleadingly suggest, as "referring to" does not, that some psychological occurrence took place.

The Polymorphous Character of Thought

So far I have tried to elaborate upon one important point about *thought*—namely, that "think" is an ambiguous word, with several distinct, but related, senses. The second important point is that each of these senses—that is, each of the concepts expressed by "think"—is polymorphous (cf. Ryle, "Thinking and Language," in *Proceedings of the Aristotelian Society,* Suppl. XXV (1951), 65–82). That is to say, "think" does not name some specific activity, result, state, possession, or disposition, of the thinker; it characterizes any one of these by relating it in certain ways to its circumstances. To seek to understand *thinking* by a close introspective or behavioral scrutiny of what we do when we think would be like seeking to understand the nature of *trying* by watching what we do when we try anything. It is not the movements, external or internal, that I make, or the ways in which I make them, when I bang the table, that allows us to call what I am doing "trying to attract attention"; it is the fact that these, or some entirely different, movements are made in certain circumstances—namely, for the purpose of making people attend to me.

Thus, although sometimes "thinking" signifies an activity in which I engage, something I can be for a while occupied in, it is not, for example, the fact that I mutter to myself about industrials and equities, or that I have mental images of columns of figures and of the stock exchange, that makes it true that "I am thinking about my stocks and shares." To be thinking about my stocks and shares is to be giving my attention, by whatever means, to matters that are relevant to my investments. I might mutter about equities while going over my part in a play; I might be thinking about my stocks and shares without muttering anything at all. Similarly, what allows me to describe what I am doing as "thinking which shares to sell" is not my saying aloud or to myself the names of my shares, or looking up the price of my shares, or having a mental picture of worked-out gold mines, but the fact that I am attempting to answer the question "Which shares shall I sell?," and that I do these various things—if I do them—as part of that attempt. Modern psychological classifications of methods of thinking do not mention the details of the examples, but solely whether trial and error or insight, focusing or scanning, was used. Again, an engine-driver can be characterized as "thinking what he is doing," not merely because he is looking at the track ahead or at the pressure of the steam, and listening to signals from his mate, but because his doing of these and other things is his way of guarding against the risks to which his journey is liable.

In a parallel fashion, the statement "I suddenly thought of my diamonds" indicates what came to my mind at a particular time, whether as the result of puzzling or by direct association. But it does not assert that the words "my diamonds," or an image of my diamonds, came to me; merely that my attention was, at least momentarily, on my diamonds, or that they seemed to me to provide an answer to my problem. The words and images that accompany my thought are not themselves the thought, but the form that the occurrence of the thought took. How does the mere appearance of an image of a cluster of diamonds constitute thinking of my diamonds rather than thinking of my wife's diamonds? Why should the utterance of the word "diamond" be counted as thinking of diamonds, rather than thinking of the word "diamond?" It is how I take the image or word that constitutes it as my thinking of it as so and so. And how I take it is shown in what I am now disposed to do, not in what happened at the moment of my becoming disposed. "If God had looked into our minds," said Wittgenstein, "he would not have been able to see there what we were speaking of." I might think of the same thing three times in one single day and have a different experience each time.

When what we manage to think of is what we were trying to think of, it is clear that thinking of something is not merely the uttering of a word, or the appearance of an image, or any other particular occurrence, since, if such an occurrence is to be counted as thinking *of* X, then we must think *that* it is the answer to our problem. The appearance of the word or image must be related to what the Wurzburg psychologists called our *Aufgabe,* or task. There is nothing in the occurrence of the word or the image of X as such to constitute it the thought *that* X; it is the circumstances in which the experience occurs that make it true that I come to think so and so. For instance, if I am trying to think to whom I lent my copy of Descartes' *Meditations,* the occurrence of the words "It was my brother," or of an image of my brother, or my swinging round to face my brother, does not constitute an answer to my problem, unless this occurrence is the form taken by my thought that it was my brother to whom I lent it. The particular occurrence has to be the expression of coming to an opinion. To think that it was my brother, as we have seen, is to come to and to hold this opinion, and this is shown in what I am now ready to do, or in what I in fact do do. This becomes even clearer when what I am trying to think of is not some item that could occur as, for example, an image or a word—as when I am thinking how to continue a long series. What may happen here, as the experiments by the Wurzburg psychologists and the analysis by Wittgenstein have suggested, is that we just get the feeling that we can answer the problem, and then proceed

to do so. No words or images need occur. It is true, of
course, that if what I am doing is thinking what word to
use in a given passage, then it is words and images of
words that will occur to me. But it is still not the mere
occurrence of such words that makes what I am doing
serve as my thinking of what word to use, since these
words could occur to me even when I am not thinking
over this problem. In an exactly similar way, if I repeat a
word, then I utter a word. But the mere uttering of the
word is not itself the repetition of a word; for that, the
word has to have been previously uttered.

Finally, it is clear that in saying that both A and B
think that war is horrible, for example, it is not necessary
that they should formulate this opinion in the same words
or in any words, in the same images or in any images.
A and B may, indeed, speak different languages; or B may
be deficient in powers of imagery. All that is necessary is
that they should be prepared to behave in similar ways.
Nor is the thought that I have expressed in the English
words "War is horrible," confined to English, or to words
at all. Any expression with the same meaning as these
words expresses that same thought.

The idea that the various concepts expressed by the
word "think" are polymorphous is supported by the tendency in modern psychology to investigate and define
thought in terms of its functions, rather than in terms of
any experiences of which we may be conscious. Recent
philosophy and recent psychology have arrived independently at a position that is expressed by Wittgenstein as
follows: In rebuttal of the suggestion that "In order to get
clear about the meaning of the word 'think' we watch ourselves while we think (since what we observe will be what
the word means)," he replied, "But this concept is not used
like that. It would be as if, without knowing how to play
chess, I were to try and make out what the word 'mate'
meant by close observation of the last move of some game
of chess."

It is partly because the concepts of *thought* are polymorphous rather than specific that the vocabulary we use to characterize thought is often metaphorical, rather than literal. We need words that will not tie the features of the thinking to any particular one of the forms that the thinking may take. Just as we contrast the specific form that our thinking takes on a given occasion with the thinking whose form it is, so we can contrast the literal descriptions of that specific form with the metaphorical descriptions of the thinking. If, for example, our thinking takes a verbal form, then the features of the form will be linguistic, philological, and physical. We can inquire about the language, the length, the style, and the sonority of the words that occurred in it. But the description of the thinking itself ignores the details of the medium in which it was conducted, since the same piece of thinking might have been conducted in a different medium. We may ask of the thinking, but not of the verbal form, "Was it logical, confused, or wishful?" If the thinking is, for example, about how to solve a problem, what interests us are descriptions of its means and methods, its trials and errors, its successes and failures. Hence, we commonly speak about this kind of thinking in metaphors borrowed from other activities that also involve these features. We metaphorically compare the features of our thinking to the literal features of such activities as traveling (e.g., false steps, blind alleys, reaching conclusions), exploring (e.g., covering the ground, getting lost in a fog), searching (e.g., leaving no stone unturned, examining every possibility, seeing the solution), maneuvering (e.g., blocked, no way out, in a dilemma), or digesting (e.g., food for thought, chewing over an idea, assimilating it).

Further, since polymorphous descriptions of an activity relate it to its circumstances, such descriptions, unlike specific descriptions of the activity, are dependent upon our knowing these circumstances. Just as we cannot describe a specific act as a "repetition" until we discover whether the same act has occurred previously, so it may not be until the thinking is finished that we can describe the occurrence of a certain word or image as "a flash of insight," or as "the first step up the garden path," as "a failure to observe a distinction," or as "the giving of due weight to an exception." The difference between a polymorphous and a specific description of a piece of thinking is, as Ryle has shown, analogous to the difference between the history and the chronicle of a series of events. The chronicler lists the details; it is the historian who tells us what they add up to.

Philosophers and psychologists have in the past sought some specific process with which thinking could be identified. Plato said that thinking was "the soul talking to itself"; the behaviorist psychologist Watson suggested that it was sub-vocal talking; the eighteenth-century empiricist philosophers believed that thinking was the use of images; the early Wurzburg School of psychology looked for it by means of introspection. The recognition that the concept of *thinking* is polymorphous enables us to see that any such search for a specific process, verbal or otherwise, is necessarily fruitless. It would be like looking for a common activity in all instances of repetition.

For the same reason, the problem of how thought is related to its expression—e.g., how my thinking about a problem is related to my talking out loud or to myself about it, or how my thought that there will be a war is related to my silent or voiced assertion that there will be a war—is not the problem of how one (internal or mental) process is related to another (external and consequent) process. It is how the polymorphous description of an activity or state is related to the description of the specific form it takes. Because we can talk without thinking, as when we babble or parrot, and we can think without talking, as when we paint or compose or construct with our hands, it follows that thinking cannot be identified with the talking that is, on this occasion, its mode of expression.

Traditionally, however, philosophers and psychologists have wrongly concluded from this that thinking is some process specifically different from talking, which may or may not accompany the talking. This answer wrongly identifies the relation between the polymorph and its specific form with the relation between two accompanying specific processes. It regards talking without thinking and thinking without talking as being like talking without gesticulating and gesticulating without talking. But to talk without thinking or to think without talking is not to engage in one specific activity without the other. To talk without thinking is to engage in one specific activity that, under the circumstances, does not amount to thinking; to think without talking is to engage in some specific activity other than talking that, under these circumstances, does amount to thinking. Talking without thinking and thinking without talking are analogous to talking without trying to attract attention and trying to attract attention without talking. To try to attract attention without talking is not to continue one of the activities I was previously engaged in and drop the other, as when I gesticulate without talking; it is to use another medium in order to do what I was previously doing. Similarly, to think without talking is to think by using another medium such as writing or drawing. Since by far the commonest form that human thinking takes is talking, the concepts of *thinking* and *talking* are in close connection, but since the form that something takes is quite different from that which takes the form, the concepts of *thinking* and *talking* are, as Wittgenstein observed, of quite a different kind.

An exactly similar point arises in the explanation of the distinction between the thought that someone holds and the words in which he expresses that thought. Certainly, the thought cannot be identified with its expression: for the same thought can be expressed in different words, thoughts are sometimes not expressed in words at all, and words sometimes express no thoughts. But it does not follow from this that thoughts are particular, perhaps mental, entities, that are sometimes accompanied by words and sometimes not, that thoughts are something naked, which we clothe before we exhibit them in public. For to say that different words express the same thought is to say that different words are doing the same job; to say that some-

one has thoughts that he is not expressing is to say that
he would, in certain circumstances, do something that he
is not actually doing; to say that such and such words express no thoughts at all is to say that they are simply not
doing a certain type of job.

CHAPTER 5

Feeling

Human nature is commonly divided into its intellectual and its emotional sides. The usual contrast to thought is feeling. Like thought, feeling is a prime matter of concern both to psychologists and to philosophers of mind. And, like the word "thought," "feeling" is a word that can mislead us into assimilating several distinct concepts, if we overlook the variety of its uses (cf. Ryle, "Feelings" in *The Philosophical Quarterly* I (1951), 193–205). The psychologist Titchener, when confronted by the enormous variety of the uses of "feeling," concluded that "there is little hope, one would think, of turning them to strict psychological account, and of giving them a place in a list of technical terms." Yet it is only by carefully sorting out the different concepts expressed by this ambiguous word that we can hope to make a fruitful start on a range of problems both in the philosophy and in the psychology of human nature.

Intellectual Feeling

First, consider a sense of "feeling" which is akin to that sense of "think" that indicates the possession of an opinion. I may either feel or think that there is a fault in your argument, that the culprit should be given a second chance, or that exercise would do me good. I can come

to or cease to feel or to think that any of these things is
so, or I may be unable to help feeling or thinking that it
is so. I can either feel or think, rightly or wrongly, that it
is so. What we think and what we feel are the same sort
of thing—namely, *that* so and so is the case. We cannot,
in this sense, ask "How do you feel?" any more than we
ask "How do you think?" Nevertheless, to feel that so and
so is the case is not exactly the same as to think that
something is so. We can feel, but not think, vaguely or
strongly, whereas we can think, but not feel, wisely or
foolishly. We can be inclined to think, but we cannot be
inclined to feel, that something is so. To ask why someone
thinks that something is so is to ask for his reasons; to ask
why he feels that it is so can only be to ask for the aspects
of the matter that cause this feeling.

A strong feeling that justice has been done may imply
a belief that it has been, but a vague feeling that something is wrong implies only doubt or suspicion; it may or
may not be succeeded by a definite belief that it is wrong.
Where we feel, however strongly, that something is so, we
are dealing either with something that is not susceptible
to rigorous proof—as in matters of taste, opinion, or
evaluation—or with what we ourselves do not yet have
such proof for. This is why we cannot sensibly be asked for
our grounds or evidence for feeling it, as we can for our
grounds or evidence for thinking it. Reasons of logic can
be demanded when we express the view that an argument
is fallacious, but not when we express only our dissatisfac-
tion with or worry about it. We can say that arguments
are fallacious because . . . , but not that arguments "smell
fishy" because. . . . We may either feel or think that 67
is too old a retiring age for academics, but we can only
think, not feel, that 67 is the present retiring age. Yet,
although we cannot ask for the grounds for a man's feeling
that there is something wrong, as we can ask for the
grounds for his thinking that there is something wrong,
we can properly put more trust in some people's feelings
than in those of others. We know that some people's feelings are more likely than those of others to be justified by

the facts, either because they have more experience in these matters, or because they are sensitive to certain clues, or because they are not easily impressed or deluded.

Such a feeling may give rise to a belief, but it is not itself a belief. It is more like a felt inclination to believe. We feel that so and so is the case because we are affected in regard to it in ways that we may not be able to pin down. We feel that there is a fault in the argument because something about it worries us; we feel that the culprit should be given a second chance because several aspects of the case leave us unhappy about condemning him. It is in this area that such forms of acceptance or rejection as hunches, intuitions, and suspicions play their part.

Perceptual Feeling

In addition to its use in the field of thought, "feeling" also has several interrelated uses in the perceptual field. In this field, "feels" does at least three different jobs for our sense of touch, whereas each of our other four senses has a different word to do each of these different jobs.

First, just as we look for something with our eyes and listen for it with our ears, so we feel for it with our fingers or other parts of the body. We can feel in our pockets for the missing bus ticket or feel underneath the table for any protruding nails. Such feeling, like looking, can be continuous or interrupted, systematic, careful, successful, or unsuccessful.

Secondly, just as we may see or hear something, whether or not we were looking or listening for it, so we may feel something, whether or not we were feeling for it. I may feel the bus ticket in the corner of my pocket, or the protruding nail under the table. Similarly, I may suddenly feel a gun in my back, or a chair against my shin. I may feel my teeth chattering, my heart thumping, or my hand trembling. In this sense, we can feel something clearly or distinctly, we can manage or fail to feel it, we can be mistaken about what we feel, or even whether we feel anything—but we cannot feel what is not there to be felt. This use of "feel," like the corresponding use of "see" or "hear," can be extended by the addition of a propositional clause—that is, one that starts "feel that"—to indicate not merely that something has been perceived, but that the agent realizes what has been perceived. Thus, a man can be said to see or feel a Confederate dollar without realizing that he has done so, but he cannot be said to see or feel that it is a Confederate dollar unless he has realized it. To feel that the object is a dollar implies feeling a dollar, feeling a dollar does not imply feeling that it is a dollar. Furthermore, we can sometimes specify what made us realize what the object was. I may have felt that it was a Confederate dollar by the peculiar milling on its edge. Nor is this use of "feeling that" the same as the intellectual use mentioned in the first section of this chapter. I may feel, in the intellectual sense of "feel," that exercise would do me good, although in fact it would not; but I cannot feel—in the perceptual sense of "feel"—that this is a Confederate dollar, unless it is. Further, feeling that it is a Confederate dollar, like seeing that it is, is the exercise of a skill. One gets to know something by using one's fingers and from clues. But no question of ability arises in merely feeling that exercise would do me good; it is not an acquisition of knowledge, but at most a correct or incorrect belief. "Can you feel whether it is a dollar?" makes sense; but "Can you feel whether exercise would do you good?" does not.

A third perceptual use of "feel" is to indicate the way in which something appears to our sense of touch. Just as a car we see may look blue, and a bell we hear may sound loud, so a radiator we feel may feel hot or smooth. It may feel so irrespective of whether it is so, just as a gray bus may look blue. Nor need my hand feel hot when the radiator feels hot to my hand, any more than my hand need feel rough when the radiator feels rough to my hand. Indeed, it may be because my hand feels cold that a luke-warm radiator feels hot to my hand. If the radiator feels painfully hot, the pain is in the hand that touches it and not in the radiator, although the heat is in the radiator and not in the hand that touches it. Just as other perceptual terms, such as "looks" or "sounds" and "sees" or "hears," may be used of the veridical or of the illusory, delusory, and hallucinatory, what "feels" so may also be illusory or imaginary. For a few minutes after the removal of a tight hat, I may feel as if there were still a hat on my head. A man in delirium tremens may not only "see" pink rats, he may "feel" spiders crawling over his face.

In the same way that a radiator may feel hot to my hand, my brow or your brow may feel hot to my hand, but to say that my brow itself feels hot, or that I feel hot, is quite different from this. I, who feel hot, may not feel hot to anyone or anything, while a radiator, which feels hot to someone, does not itself feel hot. My brow could feel hot to my or your hand, even though my brow itself did not feel hot. The brow of feverish patients often feels clammily cold. Putting my hand on my brow is, to be sure, a way of finding out whether my brow feels hot, in the sense in which a radiator feels hot. It is a mistake, however, to suppose that, when my brow feels hot, in the sense in which I feel hot, then this is a way of discovering the heat of my brow, alternative to my putting my hand on it or using an instrument such as a thermometer. Feeling hot in one's head is not an example of finding anything out. It is not, therefore, an example of finding it out without instruments or organs, as one may find that one's teeth are chattering, or that one's left hand is trembling, without using instruments or organs. A doctor finds out whether my brow is hot by feeling it; he does not ask me whether, in this sense, it is hot, although he may want to know from me whether it feels hot. I might say that my head feels hot, but not, in this sense, that I feel that it is hot— nor, therefore, that I can (or cannot) feel whether it is hot. The question of whether the radiator or my brow is hot is different from the question of whether it feels hot to my hand, and there may be criteria for deciding the former. But no distinction can be drawn between the question of whether I feel hot and the question of whether I am hot. It makes no sense to inquire whether I am mistaken in thinking that, in this sense, I am hot, or to suggest that perhaps I "only feel hot."

Feeling as a Sensation

The use of "feel" in "I feel hot" takes us away from the perception of bodies into bodily sensations, such as itches, twinges, tickles, and pains. In perceptual feeling, what is felt is not a feeling, but a perceptual object. What I feel is a nail, or the heat of the radiator, or a trembling hand; I do not feel a feeling of any of these. But, just as there is no difference between "being" hot and, in this sense, "feeling" hot, so there is no difference between being sore or itchy or in pain and feeling this way. Nor is there any difference between "feeling" itchy or ticklish and "having" an itch or a tickle. Itches or tickles cannot exist unfelt, as coins or nails can, any more than there can be unstruck blows or unmade catches. Since there is no criterion for the existence or nature of a sensation other than its being felt, we cannot sensibly ask whether a sensation might be other than it feels, as we can ask whether the heat of a radiator might be other than it feels. A sensation, unlike a coin, is not an object felt; it is, therefore, neither a public object nor a private one, whose real characteristics might be contrasted with its felt characteristics. Just as what I feel when I feel hot in the head is not the same as what I feel when, by using my hand, I can feel that my head is hot, so what I feel when I feel a sensation, such as an itch or a tickle on the back of my hand, is not something I could alternatively feel with my other hand, in the way in which I could feel a hair on the back of my hand. Nor is the itch something that could feel so and so to my other hand, when I put the other hand on the spot where the itch is. I cannot feel for and either manage or fail to feel the sensation. Feeling a sensation is not feeling some kind of perceptual object. To feel an itch is to feel itchy, but to feel a coin is not to feel coiny. We feel sensations *in* a part of our body, not *with* a part of our body. Although bodily sensations, such as itches, tickles, and pangs, are something we feel to be somewhere, either in a particular part of or all over our body, nevertheless an itch in my hand is not like a twitch in my hand. We can properly say that we feel a sensation "in our leg," even though we no longer have a leg; just as we can properly say that we feel hot in the head, even though our brow feels cold to our touch. It is part of the notion of feeling a bodily sensation that we should feel it to be somewhere, even when there cannot be anything in the place where we feel the sensation to be. This sounds paradoxical only if we wrongly persist in thinking of the sensation felt as a sort of (perhaps private) object about whose location we might be mistaken, or think of feeling it as a sort of detection, like feeling where the nail is—that is, if we assimilate locating a sensation to locating a perceptual object. Ordinarily, of course, there is something where we feel the sensation—namely, the cause of the sensation. It is in order to locate the cause of the sensation that we ask a child, "Where does it hurt?" But this does not mean that to speak of the sensation as being "in my leg" means that the cause of the sensation is in my leg; for it may be that I will still feel a sensation "in my leg," if you touch some other part of the same nerve. Sensations arrive already, though sometimes misleadingly, hallmarked "in such and such a part of our body," in contrast to the way in which we have to diagnose what they are sensations of, whether of sciatica or of fear.

Bodily sensations may be faint or acute, momentary or long continued, internally or externally caused. They may be symptoms of some more general condition, such as rheumatism, sciatica, hunger, anxiety, or fear, but they do not themselves have symptoms. They may involve a felt inclination to do something, such as scratching, flinching, grimacing, or turning away. They are described in the public language with which we describe perceptual feelings. We feel as if a pin or a red hot needle were sticking into us, as if we were burning, as if there were a fly on our arm, or as if something were chafing our neck. That is, we feel as we do feel when these things are happening, even though we know they are not and have no inclination to think that they are.

The feeling, or having, of bodily sensations has always interested philosophers, primarily because it seems to be something of which the possessor, and he alone, may be indisputably sure. It is commonly held that (1) I cannot fail to know whether I have a bodily sensation; (2) I cannot possibly know whether someone else has a bodily sensation; (3) both of these are true because each of us has a means of finding out about his own bodily sensations that is open to no one else—namely, by feeling them. The first belief has seemed to many philosophers to give a firm basis upon which our knowledge of the world around us, including the existence of other people, must be built; the second belief has been one of the commonest tenets in skeptical philosophies.

Now it is certainly, because logically, true that only I can feel my bodily sensations, since if you could feel anything when I had them—perhaps by being wired up to my nerves—what you would feel would be feelings of your own—no matter how closely they corresponded—but not mine. But is it true that my feeling my sensations is a means of my coming to know that I have them? Since, as we saw, there is no difference between feeling a sensation and having it, it would follow on this view that my having a sensation is a means of my coming to know that I have it.

Furthermore, the whole idea of *means* of my getting to know whether I have a sensation is curious. It makes no sense to ask me how I got to know whether I have a twinge, what means and methods I used, whether they were reliable or unreliable, or to ask whether I might have made a mistake and have been led by my evidence to think that I had a twinge when I had not. I cannot have evidence, good or bad, conclusive or inconclusive, of this or any other kind, for my having a bodily sensation, because I cannot have evidence for it at all. Hence, I cannot have better evidence than you have. I do not suddenly discover that I have a terrible pain in the chest, although I may suddenly notice the pain.

Far from my being able to have evidence for my sensations, it is only someone else who can have evidence for them. Only another person can have good or bad, conclusive or inconclusive evidence. When he has conclusive evidence, as he may often have, then he knows that I have these sensations. The logical fact that he is debarred from feeling my sensations does not debar him from a source of evidence about my sensations, since feeling is not here a source of evidence at all. It is not by watching myself as I grimace and writhe, or as I smile and coo, that I discover what sensations I am having; I do not discover this at all. These are the methods, however, by which I often discover that others have these same sensations. Contrariwise, others cannot feel my sensations by closing their eyes or ears and concentrating their attention on my sensations. We cannot, therefore, contrast, in the traditional way, the allegedly infallible means by which I discover whether I have a sensation and the admittedly fallible, but not inevitably mistaken, means by which I discover whether other people have sensations. One does not either discover by feeling or feel by discovering.

On the other hand, it would be wrong to conclude, as did Wittgenstein, that because no question of investigation, evidence, discovery, means, method, or mistake can arise with regard to our own sensations, we cannot therefore be said to know that we have a certain sensation. In feeling a sensation, we do not discover it; we become conscious of it, or become aware of it, or we notice it. To be conscious of a sensation is to know that one has it, just as to be conscious of a noise or a light is to know that it is there; nevertheless, we cannot ask how or by what methods someone became conscious or aware of something. We become conscious of noises and lights by hearing and seeing them and of sensations by feeling them. But feeling, like seeing and hearing, are themselves forms of consciousness, not means to it. "I know I am in pain because I feel it" is analogous to "I know there is a pen in the drawer because I see it"; while "I know he is in pain because I can see him crying" is analogous to "I know there is a pen in the drawer because I can see the ink dripping on the floor." We become conscious of our own sensations, but do not discover them; we discover the sensations of others, but we do not become conscious of them. My knowledge of the sensations of other people is a knowledge that I acquire by various means; my knowledge of my own sensations is knowledge that I receive in feeling them.

Sometimes we speak metaphorically of feeling a glow of pride, a twinge of conscience, a pang of remorse, or a stab of pity. The force of this metaphor is to indicate the momentary occurrence of some expression—not necessarily bodily—of a general condition. Just as a twinge in my back may be diagnosed as rheumatism, or a stab in my chest as heartburn, so the sudden thought that I have been unfair to a rival may be a twinge of conscience, and the urge to hold out a helping hand to a beggar may be a stab of pity. What makes either the sensation or the sensation-like feeling an expression of some condition is not its own peculiar characteristics, which may be the same when it indicates quite a different condition, but its relations, causal and otherwise, to other factors, the composition of which is that condition.

Feeling as an Inclination

A link between feeling—which is often thought of as something inner, passive, and receptive—and behavior—which is outward, active, and acquisitive—is provided by the use of "feel" in "feel inclined to do so and so." We saw above that some bodily sensations have this link with behavior. To feel an itch involves feeling inclined to scratch; to feel a tickle involves a felt inclination to giggle or to laugh. A felt inclination to do something is, indeed, often called an itch, urge, or impulse to do it. Such inclinations admit of degrees and of duration; they may be followed, succumbed to, or resisted. Having such an inclination is the same as feeling it. Like sensations, such inclinations cannot exist unfelt and hence cannot be something of whose nature or existence we could be ignorant or in doubt. It makes no sense to say that I feel inclined to do something but am not sure what it is I feel inclined to do.

The absence of any distinction between the existence of an inclination and the feeling of it is sometimes overlooked because of a confusion between this felt inclination, which is akin to temptation or "feeling like" doing something, and that inclination, which is merely a proneness to do certain kinds of things. These two inclinations are of a quite different kind. One can feel inclined to do what one never in fact does do, whereas to have a proneness to do so and so is to do it frequently. I could feel inclined (tempted) to commit suicide, but I could not very well be inclined (prone) to do it; while I could be prone to suffer accidents, I could not feel inclined to suffer them. One could have a proneness of which one was quite unaware, but one could not feel tempted to do something without knowing that one was so tempted. The inclinations that are pronenesses may in some cases be traits of character—such as punctuality, politeness, honesty, conceit, timidity, or tactlessness; but traits of character are not kinds of feelings. We do not feel polite or punctual, timid or tactless. Felt inclinations, on the other hand, like sensations, are often the expressions of what I shall later call "feelings of general condition," especially those of which it makes sense to say that one is full of or bursting with them, just as a balloon that is filled to bursting is on the brink of explosion. Fear, indignation, hope, anxiety, tenderness, pity, curiosity, interest, laughter, joy—these are typical examples of conditions that express themselves in felt inclinations. Thus, to feel indignant is to feel inclined to protest; to feel afraid is to feel like taking measures of avoidance or prevention; to feel interested is to feel inclined to pay attention. The psychologist McDougall, indeed, defined such feelings as fear, anger, and curiosity —which he called "emotions"—as "felt impulses to action."

Feelings of General Condition

There is a whole host of feelings, very different from any of the above and often subtly different from each other, that are most commonly thought of whenever "feeling" or even "emotion" is mentioned. These have been called "feelings of general condition." They include *bodily feelings*, such as feeling sleepy, wide awake, fidgety, hungry, or seasick; *moods*, such as feeling depressed, irritable, melancholy, frivolous, jovial, or happy; *emotions*, such as feeling pity, fear, pride, admiration, anger, indignation, or shame; *agitations*, such as feeling startled, shocked, excited, amazed, or flabbergasted; and what I shall call *completions*, such as feeling fit, well, tranquil, confident, content, satisfied, bored, fed up, or full.

These feelings of general condition often have bodily sensations—and even unfelt physiological changes—or their metaphorical counterparts as expressions. Sensations, both literal and metaphorical, are often diagnosed as being of such and such condition. We can have qualms of conscience as well as qualms of sea-sickness, stabs of pity as well as stabs of rheumatism, a glow of pride as well as a glow of health. But these general conditions are not themselves sensations or sensation-like occurrences. They are not locatable in some one part of our body or all over it. I do not feel fear in my tongue, although my tongue may be paralyzed with fear. These are not occurrences that could attract my attention, as a twinge of toothache or remorse can. I cannot feel deep grief for a moment, as I can feel a momentary stab of grief. I can feel in the same condition for a few days or months, but I cannot feel the same twinge, throb, or stab for more than a moment. I could have a particular itch in my fingers and not feel greedy, or I could feel greedy without feeling any itch in my fingers.

Such feelings, as I have already mentioned, frequently involve a felt inclination. When we feel afraid, we may feel inclined to make avoiding movements; when we feel tired, we may feel like lying down; when we feel frivolous, we may feel like behaving in a silly way. Since these felt inclinations to action naturally give rise, if unimpeded, to the action itself, people who feel in one of these conditions are in fact prone to exhibit certain behavior, even though at other times they manage to withstand the felt inclination. Feeling in a certain condition, therefore, commonly involves feeling certain sensations and certain inclinations, and behaving in certain ways; for various reasons, one or another of these aspects of the general condition—especially the first and the third—may be absent when the feeling is present.

A very important way in which feeling in some general condition differs both from feeling such and such a sensation, and from feeling inclined to do so and so, is how it is related to the knowledge of the sufferer. By contrast with sensations and felt inclinations, there is no reason why a person in one of these conditions should know— much less, know better than others—what he feels. We are not necessarily the best, let alone the only, diagnosticians of our own condition. Because someone feels inclined to behave in a particular way, has particular thoughts and, perhaps, also feels certain sensations, he may think he feels indignation at a certain suggestion, when it is really anger. He may think that he feels admiration, when it is envy he feels; love, when it is pride; or melancholy, when it is depression. Both ordinary life and the case histories of Freudian psychology are filled with such misconstruings. Further, not only is it proper to speak of the means by which a man comes to know of his own feelings of envy, love, or pride—as it is not proper to speak of the means by which he learns of his bodily sensations—it is also true that these means are basically the same as the means by which others get to know of them— namely, by observing the forms that their expression takes. With feelings of general condition, differently from sensations and inclinations, there is a proper contrast between feeling so and so and knowing what you feel. There is, similarly, a difference between, for example, feeling angry or envious, and feeling that one is angry or envious. Some people who feel angry or envious not only do not realize that this is so, but quite sincerely and even strongly feel that they are really unperturbed or full of admiration. Because of a tendency to lump together different sorts of feelings, philosophers have commonly taken either one extreme view—that both bodily sensations and general conditions can be known only, or best, to their possessor— or the other extreme view—that both sorts of feelings are similarly discoverable by all.

One reason for the skeptical position, that we cannot know whether another person feels in a certain condition— e.g., angry or ashamed—is the suggestion that all we ever see are external signs, which may or may not be real symptoms of the condition. Certainly, if violent trembling, profuse sweating, gesticulating, shouting, and banging the table were signs of anger, then we could legitimately contrast them with the anger itself, and say that we observed only the signs of anger. But such behavior may be the form that the anger takes. We can see anger in a man's face, not just the signs of anger. Hence, although there is a difference between an expression of anger and anger itself, this is not the difference between a sign and what it is a sign of, but between a form and what it is a form of. A violent trembling or shouting may be an expression of something other than anger, so that one can be wrong about whether someone is angry, just as one can be wrong about whether oneself is angry. But the mistake is not that of inferring wrongly the existence of some cause of the alleged signs. It is the mistake of misinterpreting the expressions—just as one may misinterpret someone's action as the making of a gift, when it was really only the offer of a loan. What makes it a misinterpretation may be that the interpreter's expectations and possible predictions of certain further behavior are mistaken. Trembling and shouting is the form, or part of the form, that one's anger often (but not necessarily always) takes; it is not the effect of one's anger.

Philosophers sometimes become muddled here because

of a failure to see a further distinction—namely, that between behavior that is, on a given occasion, the expression of fear and fear-like behavior. They first argue, quite legitimately, that the fear a man feels cannot be identified with his fear-like behavior, since not only can it be that a man who feels afraid need not show any fear-like behavior, but it can also be that a man who shows fear-like behavior need not feel afraid: he may be acting. But then our philosophers confuse this correct argument with the following erroneous one. They argue wrongly that the fear a man feels cannot be identified with the fear that he shows, and which others see, and that this is so not only on the grounds that a man who feels afraid need not show his fear, but also on the grounds that a man who shows his fear need not feel afraid. The second of these grounds is, however, mistaken. Although fear-like behavior is possible without fear, behavior that is the expression of fear is not possible without fear. I could see fear-like behavior, but not fear behavior, on the part of a man who felt no fear; for, if he in fact felt no fear, then his fear-like behavior would not be the expression of his fear. One cannot show fear, however, and yet not be afraid. The fear that a man shows, if he does show his fear, is the fear that he feels, even when he himself does not recognize his feeling as fear.

To admit, as I have, the possibility of feeling in a certain condition and not knowing what condition one is in, is not, however, to admit a contrast between feeling in a certain condition and being in that condition. For it is equally possible to be in a certain condition and not to know what condition one is in. Usually there is no difference between feeling and being in a certain condition—e.g., between feeling and being sleepy, depressed, angry, or confident. Nor do the discoveries of Freudian psychology disprove this. For an unconscious fear or hatred is not a fear or hatred that you have but do not feel; it is a fear or hatred that you both have and feel, but do not recognize as such. You have and feel certain inclinations and sensations, yet do not realize that these are the expressions of fears and hates of a certain kind. One may feel envy or jealousy without feeling—or thinking, much less knowing —that one is envious or jealous.

Nor should feelings of general condition be assimilated, as earlier philosophers thought they could be, to perceptual feelings. We do not feel anger, or shame, or remorse, with an inner sense analogous to the outer senses with which we feel a coin or a nail. Anger is not an object felt, as a coin is an object felt. To feel anger or shame is to feel angry or ashamed; to feel a coin or a nail is not to feel coiny or naily. We do not feel shame indistinctly or clearly, as we feel a coin indistinctly or clearly, nor do we succeed in feeling anger, as we succeed in feeling a nail. Feelings of general condition—like sensations, but unlike perceptual feelings—have natural facial and bodily expressions. To become aware of one's anger is to become aware of a feeling; to become aware of a coin is to become aware, perhaps by feeling with one's fingers, of an object. To feel what another feels, when it is great indignation, is to have the *same kind of* feeling; to feel what another feels, when it is a nail under the table, is to feel the *same specific* object.

A similar false assimilation of emotion to perception underlies one version of the view of the psychologist William James—namely, that an emotion is the feeling of the bodily changes that follow the perception of the object of the emotion. According to James, to feel afraid of a bear is to feel oneself trembling when one sees the bear, and to feel sorry is to feel the tears that flow when one learns of some misfortune. Although it is true that in great fear we do often feel our heart pounding and our limbs trembling, these bodily feelings cannot be picked out as the feeling of fear. We feel acutely or terribly afraid, but it is clearly or unmistakably that we feel our heart pounding. Sometimes, on the other hand, James seems to have made the different mistake of equating the emotions with sensations, because he thought of the feeling of these bodily changes as a sort of sensation, rather than as a perception.

Finally, it is worth examining some of the distinctions among the many kinds of feeling that have been grouped under this broad title of "feelings of general condition." Different philosophers and psychologists group and name these in different ways.

COMPLETIONS

Fit, well, tranquil, confident, content, satisfied, bored, indifferent, fed up, full, or empty—these are states that I can be said to feel perfectly, completely, absolutely, altogether, not quite, or not entirely; but not to feel acutely or intensely, faintly or vaguely. These are, therefore, something with a possible upper limit toward which I can tend, a terminus that I can reach. Ill, unwell, troubled, doubtful, discontented, unsatisfied, or interested, on the other hand, are feelings with an indefinite possibility of degrees. No matter how ill, doubtful, discontented, or interested I feel, it always makes sense to say that I could feel more so. There is no such thing as perfect doubt, absolute worry, complete interest. The reason for this is that each of these "completeness" feelings consists essentially in a lack of its opposite. Doubts and diseases may increase indefinitely, so that I feel more and more unsure or unwell, but they can decrease only to zero. As they decrease—that is, as I feel less and less doubtful or unwell—so I feel more and more confident or fit; when all doubts or diseases have vanished, I feel completely confident or completely fit. Wretchedness has no bottom, but contentment can be reached. It was such an attainable contentment, as opposed to limitless joy, that the Epicureans counseled in their doctrine of *ataraxia*—that is, imperturbability or peace of mind, the feeling that consists in lack of feeling, the pleasure that is lack of pain. Of the same kind also was the Skeptics' advocacy of complete indifference to all things. To feel in any of these "completeness" ways is to feel in varying degrees (fairly, quite, entirely, completely) free from the opposite feelings.

AGITATIONS

To feel startled, shocked, excited, amazed, flabbergasted, horrified, grief-stricken, convulsed, or thrilled is to feel, in one or another way, disturbed by something that has happened. We may be shocked, excited, or thrilled by what we hear, what we see, or what we realize. Psychologists often categorize such feelings as "stirred-up (or disturbed) states" and call them "emotions"; the dictionary defines "emotion" as an "agitation of mind, an excited mental state." People who are prone to such agitations— that is, people who are easily thrown into one of these states by sudden events—are commonly called "emotional." I shall, however, use the word "emotion" for another class of feelings.

Agitations are unlike moods but like emotions, in that they are related to specific items. That by which one is startled, excited, or horrified is at most, however, the *cause* of one's agitation; that of which one is afraid or hopeful, or with which one is indignant or angry, is the *object* of one's emotion. Hence, one can be afraid or hopeful of something that, being in the future, does not yet exist and, therefore, cannot be a cause; one can be horrified or excited only by the present prospect of some future event, not by the future event itself. The disturbed state into which someone has been thrown who feels in one of these ways is usually sudden and violent, but it is also of short duration. It is usually due to the reception of something that is in conflict with one's previous expectancy. It may be unpleasant, like horror or grief, and hence avoided by most people; or it may be pleasant, like excitement or thrills, and hence much sought after. People who lead lives of predictable certainty often yearn for the disturbances of thrills and excitement. Agitations are upsetting and disruptive of one's normal activities; they inhibit action. I may be struck dumb with horror or grief, too startled to move, too amazed to know what to say, too excited to think straight, helpless, or convulsed with laughter. People are often quite overcome by excitement, shock, or grief. In this respect, agitations are quite the opposite of felt inclinations, which, far from inhibiting action, incline one to it.

MOODS

To feel depressed, irritable, melancholy, joyful, jovial, out of sorts, or on top of the world, is to be in a certain mood. Moods last for some while; they pervade and color one's thought and action. Indeed, to be in a certain mood is to behave and to be liable to behave in certain ways, to feel inclined to do certain things, to be the prey of certain feelings and thoughts. If you do not feel in the mood to do so and so, you do not feel like doing it. People in a certain mood are said to take a certain view—jaundiced, rosy, or embittered—of the world, although they do not necessarily or usually suffer from certain sensations. Moods, unlike agitations or emotions, are not usually linked to something specific. We feel melancholy or jovial about things in general, not about some specific object; embarrassment and fear, excitement and hope, however, have specific objects or causes. One can always ask what you were shocked by or afraid of, but not what you were jovial or melancholy about. A man who is in a certain mood may not, indeed, know what is wrong with him, much less why. His friends may diagnose and comment upon his irritability or joviality, just as accurately or as quickly as he can himself. On the other hand, a part of the form that his mood takes is the verbal expression of the mood. A man who feels fed up or depressed need not merely sigh and moan; he may say "What a life!" or "I feel completely fed up!"

EMOTIONS

"Emotion" has commonly been used to cover all sorts of feelings, at least of a non-bodily kind. It is probably of emotions that one thinks when one thinks first of feelings.

"Emotion" is the usual chapter heading for discussions of feelings in philosophy and psychology books. Individual philosophers and psychologists have differed widely over the contents of their lists of emotions. The question of whether such and such a feeling is an emotion may sometimes be purely terminological, but I think we can find some characteristics that distinguish that group of our feelings that have been categorized as "emotions." Such feelings include pity, fear, pride, admiration, anger, indignation, shame, love, hate, hope, and remorse.

An emotion is a feeling one can be full of, in the grip of, stirred, or overcome by. It is something by which one can be moved, whether by being disturbed or by being impelled to action. On the one hand, men often have their judgment clouded or warped by jealousy, indignation, or envy; on the other hand, they often act vigorously from pity, love, or hate. An emotion can vary in intensity and in duration; it may be that a mild feeling—e.g., of fear or pity, as when we are afraid that we will have to alter our plans, or when we pity the man who has to play against the champion—stirs us too little to be called an emotion. Unlike a mood, an emotion necessarily has an object. There must be answers to such questions as "What are you afraid or ashamed of, or angry at?," "For whom do you feel pity, love, or admiration?" One cannot know that one has a certain emotion and yet not know, under some description, what its object is. The identification of its object is part of the analysis of the emotion. The fear of falling off a chair is quite unlike the fear that one's political opponents will win the next election. Hence, as psychologists now realize, experiments that are designed to induce fear of falling do not enable us to isolate any specific feeling that is common to all kinds of fears. Nor is it only the need to identify the object that shows that an emotion cannot be merely a specific felt item analogous to a sensation, so that one could identify the emotion by noticing that one is feeling this item. In speaking of an emotion, reference must also be made to what psychologists sometimes call the "situational context." Whatever I feel, it cannot be pity unless it is directed toward someone whom I think to be in unfortunate circumstances. I can feel angry, but not indignant, with myself. I cannot feel hope for the past or remorse for the future. These are not empirical discoveries about the emotions; they are conceptual facts.

Unlike perceptual feelings, indignation and fear are not felt with some organ of our body or mind; they do not give us any knowledge of the outside world or of our bodies. There is no question of trying to feel, succeeding in feeling, or getting better at feeling an emotion. Unlike sensations, emotions are not localized in us, although their expressions may be localized—for instance, in our faces or our eyes. We do not feel emotions merely momentarily, although we may have momentary sensation-like feelings that can be diagnosed as those of some emotion, like a stab of pity or a twinge of remorse. Emotions necessarily have some pattern or history.

Emotions are linked to other kinds of feelings. A feeling of fear or anxiety often shows itself in bodily sensations, such as tensions, trembling, a feeling of dryness, etc., and in uncontrollable reactions, such as blushing, screaming, and gasping. Emotions also involve a felt inclination to action and, therefore, also often involve actual action. Psychologists have sometimes described emotions as felt impulses to action. It is characteristic of a man in the grip of a certain emotion to act in a certain way. People who feel pity feel inclined to help, and often do help the object of their pity; people who feel fear feel inclined to avoid, and often do take measures to avoid the object of their fear. We could not understand a man's being reputed to feel afraid of something that he did not feel inclined to avoid or avert, or a man's being said to feel ashamed for what he felt inclined to boast about. Emotions may also be linked to action in that we do not merely feel inclined to do so and so, but also feel a desire to do it. Jealousy includes the desire to remove rivals; fear, the desire to remove dangers.

Emotions also involve the feeling, or the thought, that so and so is the case. To feel resentment involves feeling, or thinking, that you have been badly treated. To feel remorse involves feeling that you have done wrong; to feel envious involves feeling that someone else is better off than you are. It is for this reason that we can ask about an emotion, as we cannot about a sensation, whether it is justified or unjustified, reasonable or unreasonable, warranted or unwarranted. If you have not been badly treated, your resentment is unwarranted; if there was ill-treatment, but it was not Mr. A's fault, the resentment may be unjustified; or if it was beyond human avoidance, the resentment may be unreasonable. Similarly, we can hold that a man ought or ought not to have certain emotions, but not that he ought or ought not to have certain sensations, in certain circumstances. For instance, he ought to feel ashamed of himself because he has behaved disgracefully, or he ought not to feel envious of a rival just because the rival has been more successful. Emotions, when they are appropriate, can nevertheless be disproportionate to the circumstances. We can ask for a person's reasons for fearing or pitying or being ashamed of something, but not for his reasons for feeling itchy or ticklish. The answer to the former question will consist in pointing out some feature of the object in virtue of which the person regards it as appropriate to feel that emotion towards it. He may, for instance, feel that the man he pities has suffered misfortune through no fault of his own.

Philosophers and psychologists, at least since the time of Descartes, have often, although not always, treated an emotion as a private mental event, analogous to a bodily sensation. They have held that its possessor has an immediate and indisputable awareness of it that is analogous to perception, and that the emotion is empirically connected with certain kinds of objects and certain types of behavior. This view, however, cannot be true because, as we have seen, it is not its intrinsic characteristics that make the emotion what it is, but its relationship to its object and to its situation. Fear of falling is unlike fear of losing an election because of what it is a fear of. The things that one feels to be so and the things that one feels inclined to do differ in the two fears; the things one does, however, need not differ in one's crying about a fall and crying about an electoral defeat. We could adequately describe a spell of crying without mentioning what we are crying about, but we could not adequately describe a moment of fear without mentioning what we are afraid of. Fear, for instance, is unlike pity in that its object need not be thought to have any necessary connection with misfortune. Nor is there any reason why a man should not be uncertain or quite mistaken about whether it is love or pride that he feels for his son, or whether it is envy or indignation that he feels at the success of a rival.

A further reason for the traditional philosophical and psychological treatment of the connection between the object of an emotion and the emotion itself as being merely contingent lies in the mistaken equation—avoided by Aristotle, by Spinoza, and sometimes by Hume—of the object and the cause of an emotion. It was thought, for example, that what a man is afraid of arouses a mental sensation in him called "fear," in the same way in which what a man touches makes him feel ticklish.

This is a natural assumption in some cases. We say of a child who is afraid of the dark that the dark arouses his fear, that it makes him feel afraid, or that he is afraid because of it. The dark, which is the object of his fear, seems to be also the cause of his fear. The psychological position here is pictured as analogous to the physical position, as, for example, when a flammable substance is set on fire by a particular agent, such as a spark. Just as there are chemical reasons why this substance should be more affected by a spark than other substances are, so there are psychological reasons why one man should feel indignant at a remark that arouses no indignation in another man. Just as it is the combination of the chemical condition of the substance with the presence of the spark that started the fire, so it is the combination of the psychological condition of the person with the occurrence of the remark that produced his indignation. Hence, since the spark is as much, although in quite a different way, the cause of the fire as is the chemical condition of the substance, so the event about which the man is indignant—that is, the object of his indignation—is as much the cause, though in quite a different way, of his indignation as is his psychological condition. Further, in the case of the chemical substance, one can answer the question "Why did it burst into flames?" by citing either its chemical structure or the presence of the spark, while one can answer the question "What set it alight?" by citing only the presence of the spark, and the question "Why should a spark set it alight?" by citing only the chemical structure. Similarly, in the case of the indignant man, one can answer the question "Why did he become indignant?" by citing either his psychological condition or the occurrence of the particular remark; one can answer the question "What aroused his indignation?", only by citing the remark, and the question "Why should such a remark make him indignant?" only by citing his psychological condition.

On the other hand, there are quite clear cases in which the object of a fear cannot be its cause and equally clear cases in which the cause of a fear cannot be its object. The object of the fear cannot be its cause in cases in which the object is non-existent or only in the future. I may be afraid of my political opponents' winning the next election, but since there does not yet, and hopefully may never, exist such a happening as this, it cannot be the cause of my fear. Nor can we escape this conclusion by saying, perhaps rightly, that it is the thought of my opponents' winning that causes me such fear. The thought of their winning is not the object of my fear: I am afraid of their winning, not of the thought of their winning. What I am frightened *of* is my opponents' winning, but what I am frightened *by* is the thought (or the dream or the prospect) of their winning. Further, if I pity a man, he is the object of my pity, even if it is his wretched condition that causes me to pity him. If I feel ashamed of what I have done, what makes me ashamed may be your reminder, or my realization, of what I did; what I am ashamed of, however, is not that, but what I have done. Finally, I may love someone who, as we say, gives me no cause to love him.

Contrariwise, the cause of one's emotion often cannot be its object. I may feel embarrassed by certain situations because I am an adolescent; or I may feel hopeful of a happy result because I am naturally sanguine, or because I have had private reassurances from a man "in the know." But it is not my adolescence that is the object of my embarrassment, nor is either my sanguine temperament or my friend's reassurances the object of my hope. Indeed, it does not make sense to say that what I hope for causes me to feel hopeful, any more than to say that what I did in the past causes me to be ashamed of it.

The cause and the object of an emotion are logically quite different, even in instances in which the same thing can be both. If I know that I feel hope or pity, I may not know why I feel so hopeful or why I feel such pity; nevertheless, I cannot help knowing what I feel hopeful of or whom I feel pity for. An unknown cause works as effectively and in the same way as a known cause, but the object of a known emotion cannot be unknown. The relationship of a cause to its effect is contingent and has to be learned; it might have been quite otherwise. As we saw, however, it is part of the analysis of any emotion that it should have a certain type of object. Further, an emotion may gradually or quickly change, without any change in its object. Our pity or scorn for a man may increase, and our fear or indignation decrease, while we continue to look at or think of him. A beautiful house may be the object of our hatred when it belongs to another, and of our pride when it becomes our own. While the object of our emotion has not changed, other factors are at work in changing the emotion. In an analogous way, the object of one's thought or one's attention—that is, what one is thinking of or giving attention to—is not the cause of one's thought or attention, even where one's attention can be said to have been caught by it. There are reasons why a man's interest should be suddenly aroused and there are topics that arouse it. But the reason for one's interest is not necessarily the topic of it.

Some emotions seem less closely linked with their objects than others, so that it is possible to see, perhaps from his face, that a man is afraid, angry, or even ashamed, without being sure what is the object of the emotion. It is natural, therefore, to inquire what he is afraid or ashamed of or angry at. Sometimes this inquiry is put in a form— namely, "Why are you afraid, ashamed, angry?"—that makes it unclear whether we are looking for the cause or the object of the emotion. One can be in a state of fear, anxiety, or pleasure, but not in a state of interest, scorn, or pity. What arouses one's pity or scorn can be only its object, not its cause; what arouses one's fear, anxiety, or pleasure can be both its object and its cause.

With other emotions, however, such as pity, admiration, hate, and remorse, it does not seem possible to know that a man feels one of these without knowing to what it is directed. Pity, admiration, and remorse, unlike fear, anger, and anxiety, cannot be thought of as general states, inducible by various means. They are specific to each object. There is, therefore, no need to ask for the object of a man's emotion, but only *why* he should feel it toward that object. Similarly, when the object of fear, anger, or shame is known, to ask why he is afraid, angry, or ashamed is to ask for the cause of the emotion. Hence, we usually seek the cause of an emotion only when we already know its object. We seek objects for unspecified emotions and causes for specified emotions. We ask "What are you afraid of?" but "Why are you afraid of that?"

CHAPTER 6

Explanations of Human Behavior

The Problem of Explanation

All of us are called upon frequently to explain our own or other people's behavior, either quite non-committally or else by way of excuse or justification. Nor is it only what we do that needs explanation, but also what we omit to do; we can be as guilty of sins of omission as of commission. Those of us, whether parents, teachers, or lawmakers, who are professionally interested in correcting and improving behavior, need first to understand it. For instance, lessons designed to correct *mistakes* are not the same as instructions drawn up to prevent *accidents*. There are professionals—the "psychologists" and "sociologists"— whose area of inquiry is the scientific explanation of human behavior.

Philosophy gives one no special competence to understand behavior, beyond any competence one may possess as a parent or a teacher, as a lawmaker or a psychologist. Its task in this field is not to explain behavior, but to explain the kinds of explanations of it that we ordinarily offer in our amateur or professional capacities. Not human behavior, but the language and concepts involved in our ways of thinking of it, are what furnish this part of a philosopher's material. A philosophy of explanation, we might say, seeks to identify, classify, and explain different kinds of explanation.

The things that may happen and the things that a person may do are very diverse; so also are the things that explain happenings and actions. The sorts of question the philosopher asks are these:

(1) Are all explanations of all things of the same kind? For instance, is a search for an explanation always a search for some antecedent of the thing to be explained, as seems to have been believed by the philosophers Hume and Mill and the majority of earlier scientists?

(2) Can certain kinds of things be explained only by certain kinds of factors? That would mean that we can, for example, have a motive for writing a letter, but not for losing one; for making someone feel miserable, but not for feeling miserable oneself. Again, is an attempt to explain human activity, by contrast with natural happenings, in terms of physical or physiological changes necessarily misconceived? Consider, for instance, the difference between explaining why certain sounds came out of a man's mouth, why he shouted, and why he shouted an order. As a corollary of this, if we characterize a certain action in a certain way—e.g., as a mistake or as a piece of carelessness or as the carrying out of an order—are we thereby anticipating or even prejudging the kind of explanation that can (logically) be given of it? Thus, the very same movement can be correctly described either as pressing button X or as starting a world war. But, while I could explain my pressing button X as done by mistake—because I had really intended to press button Y—my starting a world war can be explained as an accident, but not as something done by mistake. A *consequence*, an *effect*, and a *result*, for example, of a debate in the University Senate, require different sorts of explanations, even when the same factor, e.g., the Vice-Chancellor's intervention, explains all three.

(3) Is an explanation in terms of one kind of factor necessarily a different kind of explanation from one in terms of

another kind of factor? Conversely, do different kinds of explanations necessarily contain different kinds of factors? For instance, is an explanation in terms of antecedent events a different kind of explanation from one in terms of purpose; is an explanation in terms of mood different from one in terms of habit? Are the factors that can be said to "persuade" us to do things *eo ipso* different from those that "drive" us, and these different again from those that provide a motive for our actions?

(4) Are different kinds of explanations, or explanations in terms of certain kinds of factors, mutually exclusive? We would be inclined to say, for instance, that if a man does something because he was tempted, it may also be true that he did it because he is vain, as well as that there was a point in his doing it. On the other hand, can someone who did something because he "just felt like doing it" also have a motive for doing it, or can he have done it because he was driven to it?

(5) What, in fact, are the different kinds of factors that may appear in our explanations of human behavior?

(6) What are the kinds of explanations in which the different kinds of factors may appear?

(7) What kinds of factors and explanations are logically possible for the different kinds of things that require explanation?

The Language of Explanation

Our everyday language and thought is extremely rich in the tools it offers us for explaining what people do, precisely because there are myriad things that explain what people do. A man may wave his arms about because he has had a telephone call or a beating, because he is full of joy or has gone mad, because he wishes to attract attention or is practicing signaling, or just because he feels like it. These are different explanations of his behavior. In what way, if any, are they different kinds of explanations?

Here again the colloquial terms of our language provide us with material and with a clue. Instead of simply asking "why" someone did something, we may ask what "made" him or "caused" him or "possessed" him to do it, what "drove" him or "led" him to it, what "persuaded" or "prompted" him to do it; what was the "point" of his doing it, what was he "after," how did he "come" to do it, what was his "purpose," etc. We may do something for pleasure, but pleasure does not drive or persuade us to do things. We could not say that a thump on our back was the point of our doing something. If I do something because I do not realize what I am doing, then, even though there may be a "cause" for my doing it, nothing could be said to have persuaded me or driven me to do it; nor was there something I was after; nor could I have done it for joy. Do these linguistic facts suggest that there are fairly strict limitations on the kinds of factors that can be offered in different kinds of explanations? Do they, indeed, suggest that an explanation is of the kind it is because the factor offered in it is of the kind it is? Or, on the other hand, are these linguistic differences in the way we ask for and give explanations merely verbal, perhaps only idiosyncrasies of the English language? Both anger and reasoned argument may "make" or "cause" a man to change his mind. But does not the fact that only the argument can "persuade" him and only the anger can "drive" him, or the fact that we act "in" anger but "from" conviction, point to a difference between the kinds of explanations that anger and argument offer for our behavior?

We are provided by everyday language and thinking not only with the means for referring to particular explanations and particular factors in explanations, but also with a number of words and ideas whose job it is to classify *kinds* of explanations and the *kinds* of things that may on occasion occur as factors in explanations. First, the kinds of things that may on occasion provide factors in explanations include antecedent events, feelings, desires, moods, traits, attitudes, disabilities, inclinations, and dispositions, whether habitual or instinctive. Secondly, kinds of explanations are classified in our ordinary thought by such ideas as *reason, cause,* and *motive,* or by reference to the kinds of factors that occur in these explanations.

It is because we express in our everyday speech so many different ideas of and about explanation that a philosopher who is interested in the nature of explanation must pay close attention to what we actually say—that is, to our "ordinary language." The use of one general term, whether non-technical, such as "cause" and "spring of action," or technical, such as "motivation" and "drive," instead of many colloquialisms, such as "lead," "induce," "point of," "intention," and "for the sake of," tempts one to think that all explanations are of the same kind.

Kinds of Explanations and Factors in Explanations

Failure to see the difference between an idea whose job is to classify kinds of explanation and an idea whose job is to classify those things that may appear as factors in an explanation has been a source of confusion in psychology and philosophy, particularly about the nature of *motive* and *desire.*

The words "reason," "motive," and "cause" do not refer to anything that could be a factor in an explanation of conduct, in the way that an antecedent event, a feeling, a habit, or an instinct could operate as such a factor. And this despite the fact that there is a sense in which the agent himself can be correctly said to "have" a reason or a motive. Reasons, motives, and causes, unlike events, do not happen at particular times or places; unlike feelings, they cannot either titillate or torment us, they cannot be either faint or acute; unlike inclinations, they cannot be thwarted by the world; unlike attitudes, they cannot be acquired by practice, nor could we be born with them, as we are born with instincts. "Reason," "motive," and "cause" are words that are used to indicate kinds of explanations. Unlike anything that could be a factor in an explanation, reasons, motives, and causes can be "plausible," "ulterior," "main," or "subsidiary." Discovering the reason why a man did something is not itself discovering his feelings or his attitudes, his moods or his habits, although some of these may provide the reason.

MOTIVE AS A KIND OF EXPLANATION

Although no one, perhaps, is likely to confuse kinds of explanations with kinds of factors when he is operating with the notions of *reason* and *cause*, this confusion has been a common mistake when people are operating with the notion of *motive*. Philosophers and psychologists have disputed whether, when a deed has a motive, that motive is a feeling or an event or a tendency. Writers on ethics almost invariably make the word "motive" synonymous with "desire" or "inclination," and think of it as a kind of impulse or itch, which "moves" men to do things. Hence, they talk of "producing" or "cultivating" or "having one's mind occupied by" motives, when what they ought to speak of in these contexts is desire. Freud thought that to be unaware of your motive for an action is to have a feeling inside you of which you are unconscious. Ryle's justly famous attack on the identification of motives with feelings (impulses, mental occurences, acts, or states) is accompanied by his own identification of motives with dispositions. He shares his opponent's assumption that "motive" and "inclination" are synonymous, and really disputes only whether inclinations are feelings or dispositions. Thus, he speaks as if he were investigating the relationship of habits and moods to motives, when in fact he is discussing their relationship to inclinations.

But the concept of *motive* is logically quite different from both the concept of *feeling* (or mental occurrence, etc.) and that of *disposition*. The word "motive" signifies a kind of explanation, not a kind of factor that can occur in explanations. *Motive* is of the same logical class as *reason* and *cause*. Thus, while it is appropriate to speak of a person's feelings and dispositions when no question of explanation has arisen, the concept of *motive* has a point only within the context of explanation. Unlike feelings, motives do not occur at a particular time and place, nor are they faint or acute, pleasant or unpleasant. Unlike dispositions, motives are not acquired at birth or by practice; they are not either increased or lost; they are not taught or learned, nor are they cured.

More particularly, a motive is not a desire, despite the important logical relations between the two, which, no doubt, accounts in large part for the popularity of this identification. Unlike desires, motives cannot properly be described as momentary or lifelong, gnawing or fierce, satisfied or unsatisfied; nothing arouses or thwarts them, nor can they be cultivated, produced, or suppressed, or occupy one's mind. Both a desire and a motive must be for something; but a desire for X could furnish a motive only for doing Y, not for doing X. A man's motive for murder may be his desire for gain, but it could not be his desire to kill. Because the concept of *motive*, unlike that of *desire*, is tied to the idea of explanation, we may quite straightforwardly speak of desiring to do things that we never do; the only sense, however, in which we can be said to have a motive for doing something we do not do is that an explanation is available of why we might have done it or might do it. Thus, if a man wants X, and Y is a means to X, then he can be said to have a motive for doing Y, whether or not he actually does Y, and whether or not the idea of doing Y actually occurs to him. The sense in which a suspect may be said to have had a motive for killing the victim whom he did not in fact kill is akin to the sense in which a long-suffering person may be said to have a reason for showing the anger that in fact he does not show.

Motives have frequently, even by recent writers on the topic, been identified with intentions. But this is the same kind of mistake as the identification of motive with feeling or disposition or desire. For to ask for a motive is necessarily to ask for an explanation for the doing of what has been or might be done, whereas to ask for a person's intentions may be only to ask what he is going to do, not why he is going to do that. One need not be aware of one's motive for doing something, whether one does it or not, but it would be strange to say of someone who intended to do something, or who had done something with intent, that he did not know what he intended to do. Further, while I may have a motive for doing something—e.g., murdering the Vice-President—which I have no intention of doing, I may intend to do something just because I want to do it, and for which, therefore, I have no motive. Nor need the intention with which I do something be the same as the motive from which I do it. Whether I buy a sailing ticket at a low price this week or at a high price next week may depend on whether my motive is greed, but my intention of going on a cruise next year is the same. A person's intentions, like his thoughts but unlike his motives, are something he can be full of, have had for a long time, form or express or announce at a particular moment, and they can be clear or firm. Intentions are put into effect or carried out; motives either operate or do not.

It is because assigning a motive is giving a kind of explanation, whereas "intention" signifies something that may appear in explanations, that we can properly say that the reason why someone did X was that he intended to do Y, while it would be a mere pleonasm to say that a motive was the reason why. A man's intention in withdrawing his bank balance might be to emigrate, but his motive could at most be a desire to emigrate. Greed, jealousy, vindictiveness, or patriotism—which can serve as motives—cannot serve as intentions. Further, one can have a motive for what one intends as much as for what one does; but one cannot have a motive for having a motive. Indeed, people who intend the same thing can have quite different motives, as when one man intends to kill for money and another for revenge.

One source of the confusion between a kind of explanation—such as the giving of a motive or a reason—and a factor in explanations—such as a desire—is possibly the fact that to name the motive or give the reason for some behavior is of course to name or offer one of the factors that can appear in explanations of the kind dealing with motive or reason. The question "What was his motive?" may be answered by referring, for example, to his ambition or jealousy or his victim's money; the question 'What was the reason?' may be answered by indicating, for example, a habit or attitude. Now, if you name a motive or give a reason by mentioning a trait, habit, attitude, or event, it is easy to suppose that that motive or reason is identical with one of these. The mistake here is the same as that made by a man who, knowing that a person's house, car, yacht, and shares are his assets, supposes that the concept of *assets* is like that of *car* or *house*. After all, if we deprive a person of some of his assets, do we not deprive him of some such things as these? It is true that assets, like cars and houses, may be acquired, lost, surrendered, or given as security. Yet the mistake is clear. Assets, unlike cars, cannot be driven; unlike yachts, they cannot either have or lack sails; unlike houses, they are not either inhabitable or derelict. *Asset* is a concept that signifies that certain material and immaterial things are advantageous possessions of the person. It is not the name of any of the possessions themselves.

FACTORS IN MOTIVE-EXPLANATIONS

My suggestion in the previous section was that the difference between *motive*, on the one hand, and such concepts as *feeling, disposition, desire,* and *intention,* on the other, is the difference between a concept that indicates a kind of explanation and concepts that indicate factors which may, on occasion, appear in explanations. I shall now consider the quite different thesis that it is the presence of one such factor—whether it be feeling, disposition, intention, or desire—that makes an explanation an explanation of the motive kind.

Obviously, the mere occurrence of a feeling is not sufficient to provide a motive for what I do. If I lash out because I am in pain, or go to bed because I feel tired, or burst out laughing because I feel like it, I do not act from a motive. Conversely, a man who works hard from ambition does not have ambitious feelings. Similarly, having a particular thought before I do something is neither a necessary nor a sufficient condition for my doing it from a motive. The thought of a juicy steak may make me hurry my morning's work, but it does not in itself provide a motive for hurrying. For, on the one hand, greed could be my motive for hurrying, even if I had no such thought. And, on the other, the thought of the steak I was going to have might make me smack my lips, and the thought of a steak I had missed might make me weep; but I do not have a motive either for weeping or for smacking my lips.

Nor do dispositions necessarily provide motives. Certainly, what a person does can be explained by reference to his honesty or considerateness, his bravery or timidity, his tactlessness or conceit. But timidity is not a motive for hesitating to answer, conceit is not a motive for undertaking jobs beyond one's competence, tactlessness is not a motive for dropping conversational bricks. What has confused philosophers here is that some dispositions—such as greed, vindictiveness, and patriotism—undoubtedly do come into play as motives. It is not, however, because they are dispositions that they can play this role, but because of their reference to action "for the sake of" something further. Otherwise, as in fact philosophers have sometimes wrongly supposed, any disposition could furnish a motive. Besides, a person can be said correctly to act from a motive, even when he has no disposition to do what he did, as when I kill a man to prevent him revealing a secret.

Philosophers commonly hold that intentions can be referred to as motives for action; but this is, I think, a mistake and arises in part from wrongly supposing that intentions, like motives, can be expressed in terms of what someone wants or desires to do. Certainly, what a person intends to do and what he wants to do frequently coincide; this, no doubt, is the cause of their assimilation. But this natural connection does not indicate any logical connection.

Sometimes people intend to do things, such as giving up a prized possession, which they do not want to do, and sometimes they want to do things, such as taking forbidden fruit, which for various reasons they have no intention of doing. But even when what we want to do and what we intend to do coincide, they are conceptually quite different and therefore provide different explanations for what we do. To say that someone is selling his house because he intends to live abroad is not to say that he is selling it because he wants to live abroad, even though both explanations may be true. One can want, but not intend, desperately, ardently, or to a particular degree; one can intend, but not want, firmly, resolutely, or fully. "I intend," but not "I want," can express determination or resolution. One can desire to do or to get something, to be or to suffer something, but one can intend only to do. To say that one intends to achieve or to be so and so is not to announce one's intentions, but to express one's determination, or to make a resolution. One can explain one's gathering of the crops in terms of either the desire or the intention to feed them to the cattle, but only in terms of a desire to beat the weather. Since, therefore, an explanation in terms of what a person intends to do is not the same as one that is couched in terms of what he wants to do, and since explanations by motives are expressible in the latter way, an intention cannot be regarded as a factor in a motive explanation.

Desires, as I have just mentioned, are logically related to motives in a way in which neither feelings, dispositions, nor intentions are. Whenever it can be said that someone acted from such and such motive, it can also be said that he wanted so and so. Greedy men want possessions, ambitious men want power, vindictive men want to get their own back, vain men want to show off, and patriotic men want to serve their country. But the converse is not necessarily true. Not every explanation in terms of want or desire is of the motive type. If a person does something just because he wants to do it, he does not act from a

motive. Further, our desires, especially when they are unsatisfied, can make us rage or sulk; but we do not ordinarily rage or sulk from a motive.

I shall try to show in a later section what kind of explanation is in fact signified by the notion of *motive*. Here
I have only argued, first, that motive has been wrongly
assimilated to various factors that may appear in some
kinds of explanations and, secondly, that many of the factors that are commonly said by philosophers to provide
motives either need not or cannot do so.

Different Explanations and Different Factors

Besides assimilating various kinds of explanations to each
other, or trying to reduce all kinds to one, philosophers
have sometimes assimilated different kinds of factors.
Those who have thought that explanations are really in
terms of an event or a happening that is antecedent to
what is to be explained have often regarded desires, intentions, inclinations, will power, and even habits and traits,
as mental events, such as feelings or thoughts, that precede and cause what is to be explained. We shall see,
however, that although an explanation in terms of antecedent events can sometimes be given of psychological
phenomena, it is not the only kind of explanation and it
does not in fact apply to the factors just mentioned.

Some instances of the assimilation of one factor to
another are quite common. Sometimes this is so because
it is thought that what holds for some members of a given
class holds for all. Because, for instance, many character
traits, such as greed, avarice, ambition, vindictiveness, or
jealousy, can serve as motives, it has been mistakenly
thought that motives are, or are necessarily provided by,
character traits. But, as we saw, to act from conceit, honesty, or timidity, unlike acting from avarice, ambition, or
jealousy, is not to act from a motive; we may try to satisfy
our ambition but not our timidity.

More commonly, however, two different factors have
been assimilated because in some or many cases they are

present together. Thus, a man usually wants to do what he intends to do, and often intends to do what he wants to do; a man who does not care what he does usually does not take any care in what he does. Often this coincidence is due to the fact that the presence of one factor is the cause of the presence of the other. The indifference of the man who does not care is often the cause of his failure to take care; it is often because people want to do something that they intend to do it. Of course, the very fact that one of the factors can be the cause of the other should warn us that these two factors are different; nothing can be its own cause. In some cases, an additional stimulus to false assimilation is provided by the accident that the two factors are signified by the same ambiguous word. Thus, we describe the man who does not care what people think as "careless" of the world's opinion, and we describe the man who does not take care in what he does as "careless."

The kinds of explanations of human behavior and the kinds of factors that can appear in such explanations are, however, very varied. Let us look at some of them.

FACTORS OF AN ANTECEDENT CAUSAL KIND

What happens to someone at a particular moment is sometimes explained by pointing to some antecedent occurrence. A man may fall forward or give a gasp because he has been thumped on the back. A similar kind of explanation is possible for what a person does, when he does it as a reaction to an occurrence, and not as a chosen course of action. Thus, people may instinctively reach for offered food, when hungry, or jump, when an unexpected noise is heard; they may blink their eyes by reflex, when a dazzling light is shone on them; they may involuntarily cry out, when hit hard; or they may automatically prick up their ears, when their name is mentioned.

Thirdly, it is often legitimate to cite antecedent events, even when what is to be explained is not merely what happened to a human being, or what he did as a reaction, but some action of his. The reception of a message

or a request, or the hearing, seeing, or touching of something, may be the occasion of my doing something. It is
the telegram announcing my success that makes me jump
for joy, the request from my neighbor that makes me pass
the sugar, the sight of the blaze that sends me rushing for
the fire extinguisher.

Fourthly, even when I act after deliberation and thought,
for reasons I have now made my own, and on a carefully
chosen course, I may refer in explanation to my colleague's
argument that persuaded me, my elder brother who in-
duced me, my business associate who bribed me, my wife's
smile that encouraged me, the threat or promise that led
me, the point that weighed most with me, or the change
of circumstances that forced me. Although there is no hint
that any of these things acted on me as one billiard ball
does on another, or as some electrical forces in my brain,
or some mental association between ideas, we can often
properly say that, but for the particular antecedent, I
would not have done what I did. We can say, in short,
that it explains what I did.

When, however, philosophers and psychologists speak
of antecedent causal explanations of human behavior, they
commonly mean, not the examples I have given above,
but certain mental or physiological entities or events,
whose alleged occurrence before the action in question is
said to explain the action. Philosophers and early psychologists proposed ideas, thoughts, desires, motives, intentions, purposes, or reasons, as candidates for the role
of antecedent cause; but our examination below of the
part these factors actually play in explaining human behavior will show that they do not, and could not, function
in this role. Here I want to show that no merely physiological antecedent could provide an explanation for those
parts of human behavior that are described as "actions"
rather than as "occurrences" or as "happenings."

The nub of the argument is the distinction, discussed in
Chapter 3, between polymorphous and specific concepts.
The same specific occurrence—e.g., playing on the piano
—may or may not, on a given occasion, also be an in-

stance of something polymorphously describable as, for example, practicing for a concert, or giving a concert recital, or trying to annoy the neighbors. There need be no difference in the specific occurrence itself to make it one of these rather than the other, but only a difference in the circumstances in which it takes place.

It is obvious that what counts as an explanation of so and so partly depends on the description given of so and so. We can explain why a man is playing on the piano by saying that he is practicing, but we cannot explain why a man is practicing on the piano by saying that he is playing it. Similarly, if we describe what a man does as making a mistake, we may thereby explain his specific deed as being due to a mistake, but we could not explain his making of the mistake in that same way.

Consider now a particular happening involving a human being. If we describe what is happening in some elementary physical terms, such as "a man's hand is moving," we might reasonably explain why this happened by reference to various physiological events and processes in his arm and brain. But if we describe exactly the same occurrence as "a man is handing a present to a friend," then, although there may occur exactly the same physiological antecedents as before—without which he could not give a present, since without them his hand would not move—we cannot explain why he handed over this present by mentioning these physiological details. Nor will it do to say that the particular circumstances that allow us to describe the specific happening of moving the hand as an instance of giving a present to a friend must include something that is itself physiological. For these circumstances may be the intention of the agent, the relation of the agent to the other man, the society's conventions about the legitimate means of giving a present, the legal consequences of this act, etc. It is implausible to suppose that all these circumstances must be correlated with physiological changes in the agent. It is not the absence of some physiological component that makes it impossible for my right hand to give my left hand a present.

We see, then, that if what happens or is done is described with a certain complexity—e.g., as giving a present to a friend—then it is no longer explicable in purely physiological terms, however necessary physiological entities and events are to its occurrence. This is only part of the wider thesis that the way in which something is described determines in part what can be offered as an explanation for it. Now, some philosophers would hold that any description of what is done that is sufficient to entitle it to be called a human action, as opposed to a mere happening, is such as to rule out a merely physiological explanation of its occurrence. For example, the moving of my hand can be explained physiologically—though it can also be explained by the description "giving a present"— only because it would not thereby count as a human action; the giving of a present, on the other hand, which is a human action, cannot be explained purely physiologically. In other words, the elements that are necessary in a description in order to make it a description of a human action—such elements as references to human society, laws, organization, needs, interests, intentions, etc.—are such as to render the deed now described inexplicable without reference to more than physiological details.

EXPLANATIONS IN TERMS OF DESIRES

Explicit explanations of human behavior in terms of what we want or desire are very common. We may do something either because we want to do it, or because we want something else. Now, what kind of explanation is given by referring to what we want or desire?

The traditional answer has been that reference to desiring or wanting provides a causal antecedent of the behavior to be explained. Although Aristotle sometimes interpreted "doing X from desire of Y" in teleological terms—namely, as an instance of being drawn to Y—he also spoke of desire as a causal antecedent that moves our limbs. So Hobbes and Hume, influenced by the mechanics of their age, modeled desire on the forces of the physicists.

Present-day psychologists and physiologists treat it as a mental or neural occurrence that precedes behavior. This antecedent causal view gains plausibility from the way we think and speak of desire as something that moves, excites, or drives us to do things, and from the common belief that in a human being's performance of an action we have the paradigm case of cause and effect. Philosophers in the past have commonly treated desire as something that is felt in somewhat the same way as a sensation is felt.

There are, however, grave difficulties involved in regarding an explanation in terms of desire as of an antecedent causal kind.

First, although desires, like sensations, can occur at a particular time, can be mild or acute, fleeting or momentary, they can also, unlike sensations, be dominating, blinding, and obsessive. They can be dormant or aroused, momentary or life-long. Further, they can exist for long periods unfelt. What those philosophers, who have identified desires with felt mental sensations, have confused is desire and the felt inclinations, the felt frustrations and the felt needs and discomforts, which are characteristic of desires that are not yet satisfied. Desire itself, however, should not be identified with any of the forms in which it is experienced. It is the pattern of these forms oriented to the object of desire, just as an emotion is a pattern of feelings and behavior oriented toward its object.

Secondly, it is characteristic of what serves as a cause that it is independent of its particular effect, in the sense that its description need not make any reference to such an effect. For instance, there is no reference to an explosion in the description of a match, although the match may on occasion cause an explosion. The description of the cause of an event *may*, of course, contain a reference to the event which is its effect, as when we explain a soldier's presenting arms because he heard the command to present arms. But hearing the command to present arms could have a different effect; and presenting arms could be due to a different cause. On the other hand, the desire that is alleged to be the cause of a particular deed is necessarily characterized either as a desire to do that deed or as a desire for something to which that deed is thought to be a means. Similarly, we cannot ordinarily say what will be the effect of a given occurrence prior to its having been seen in operation, whereas the theory before us holds that the effect, if any, of a desire to do X is necessarily the doing of X or of something which it is thought will bring about X. Further, an explanation of behavior in terms of desire describes that behavior in such a way that a causal explanation is never a description of the effect. For instance, making one's eyebrows twitch from a desire to twitch them is a manifestation of that desire; it is doing what one wants, in a way in which an explosion is not a manifestation, but an effect, of a lighted match.

A third main difference between a desire and an antecedent cause, as explanations of human behavior, is that two antecedents can be distinguished from each other independently of their possible effects, whereas we distinguish desires—e.g., a desire for X and a desire for Y—in terms of their possible effects and their potential fulfillments. Further, if a desire were an antecedent occurrence—e.g., a mental occurrence—by what means would one distinguish two such occurrences, say the desire to move one's first toe and the desire to move one's second toe? Our previous analyses of *thought* and *feeling* show that the distinction between the desire to move one's toe, the thought of moving it, and the memory of having moved it is not a distinction between various mental occurrences that are identifiable separately by introspection.

A fourth objection is that, if a desire were an antecedent occurrence, it could at most cause something to happen, but it could not cause an action of anyone. For we saw earlier that, if what happens is described as an "action," then this extra description rules out as fully explanatory that factor which was sufficient to explain what happened when it was simply described as a happening. For instance, just as what explains piano playing is not what explains practicing, even though the practicing is the piano playing under a more complex description, so the

antecedent events that are sufficient to explain certain subsequent events are not sufficient to explain the corresponding actions—e.g., they are sufficient to explain my falling,
but not my jumping. On the other hand, if a desire can
explain anything, it must explain an action, but not a happening—my jumping, but not my falling. Thus, we are in
the dilemma that, if a desire is an antecedent cause, it will
not fully explain an action, but only a happening; but if
it is a desire, it will not explain a happening, but only an
action. The way out of this dilemma is to suppose that a
desire is not an antecedent cause. "If I want to, I can
move it" is not like "If I push, I can move it." "If I push"
may indicate causal antecedent conditions of the move,
but "If I want to" indicates the absence of any internal
hindrance on my part to the move.

Philosophers have traditionally tried to distinguish between mere happenings, such as my falling, and an action,
such as my jumping, by supposing that in the latter case
the happening was preceded by a mental act, called an
"act of volition." But, apart from the fact that there is no
evidence for such an act, that its purported connection with
its alleged effect remains a mystery, and that no qualities
of acts—such as duration, method, manner, or motive—
can sensibly be attributed to it, it could not do the job
assigned to it. For, if the "volition" is an act, and not a
happening, it must, on this very hypothesis, be preceded
by another "act of volition," and so on *ad infinitum*. And
if it is itself a mere happening, it does not seem adequate
to explain the difference between action and happening.

If we must reject, then, the view that desires explain
behavior in the way in which causal antecedents explain
happenings, what kind of explanation do they give? Since,
as I indicated earlier, a desire is not something, such as a
feeling, that we may specify in isolation, but something
that can be identified only as a desire *for* this or that, what
we have to consider is not desire, but desire for X.

What kind of explanation, then, are we giving when we
say either "I did X because I wanted to do X" or "I did X
because I wanted to do Y," where the X that I did is

necessarily an action and not a happening? Only primitive superstition would try to explain happenings in terms of what people want.

Explanations in terms of desires are partly negative—that is, they indicate that there was no reason for the action other than its being a manifestation of the make-up or the current orientation of the agent. I may do something that I wanted to do; but I do not do it because I wanted to do it, if in fact I did it because I had to do it. A man who does X because he wants to do it may have just felt like doing X, or felt a need to do X, or he may have been thinking about doing X, or the idea of doing X may have appeared attractive to him; therefore, the circumstances being favorable and no objection arising, he went ahead and did X. Nothing caused him to do X, he just did it. Similarly, he may have been seeking Y, or felt a need for Y, or been asked to get Y; seeing an opportunity for doing X, which he thought to be a means to Y, he did X. He did X, in short, because he wanted Y. We explain his performance of X in the light of his character, his interests, his intentions, his pursuits, and his needs, and, sometimes, his present inclinations or thoughts—all these, as opposed to any external causes, such as physical force, orders, threats, etc. But to say that someone did so and so because he wanted to do it is not the same as saying that some prior inclination or need or thought caused him to do it. Part of what is meant by saying that a man wants to do X is that he will do it in favorable and unobjectionable circumstances. Children have to be taught that they cannot always do just what they want. A man who is doing what he wanted to do cannot still want to do it, even though he may now want to continue to do it; nor can he any longer feel inclined to do it, nor feel a need for it, nor pursue it.

LAW-LIKE FACTORS

Many present-day writers on explanation insist that to explain an event is always to ask for a general law that applies to the particular event. An elementary instance of this is our explaining something by classifying it as being of a certain kind—for example, it dissolved because it is a salt; he stutters because he is timid. The law or generalization in its turn is to be explained by subsuming it under a higher law or more general theory, and so on until everything is finally explained in a complete hierarchical system. Sometimes it is added that the statement that describes what is to be explained must be deduced from the general law, together with a premise that states that what is to be explained is an instance of the kind of thing to which the law applies. Thus, we are said to explain why the rod in my hand expanded when we argue that "Metal expands when heated; this rod is metal; therefore this rod expanded when heated." Other philosophers do not insist on deduction, but accept something as being explained when it can be shown to fall, in some more vague way, under a given law.

It is significant that advocates of this view of explanation are influenced mainly by examples from the advanced sciences, which are characterized partly by their systematic form and partly by their predictive capacity. It is of the nature of science to look for laws that are applicable to particular cases. The law explains the particular event by showing that it is an example of a series of events, any one of which would have happened in the same circumstances, and all of which can, therefore, be predicted from knowledge of this law. The law links the particular to the general, the normal, or the invariable.

Without discussing here the large question of whether explanation is necessarily in terms of laws or generalizations, I shall give a few examples of concepts that we commonly use to give a law-like explanation of human behavior.

Habit. One of the simplest explanations of what a person does—so simple as sometimes to feel rather unsatisfying—is to attribute it to habit—to say that it was due to habit or done from force of habit, or just that "It's a habit." Only a type, not a single piece, of behavior can be described as a habit or as habitual. A man may have a habit of scratching his head, but not of scratching his head on his thirtieth birthday. A habit cannot be interrupted or take a certain time to complete, although its beginning ·and its end may be roughly dated.

Either a type or a piece of behavior is, however, explainable as a habit, habitual, or due to habit. My opening the window each morning when I enter my study and my opening it on this particular morning may both be put down to habit. But the explanation is of a logically different kind for the single case and for the type of case. For, since my opening my window each morning is describable as a habit, that explanation merely rules out any other—such as that I like fresh air or that I have my orders. But since opening the window on a particular occasion is not describable as a habit, the explanation in terms of habit does add something.

To say that a type of behavior is a habit or is habitual is to say that instances of it occur regularly, almost invariably. We say both "I make a habit of" and "I make a practice of"; both "I am not in the habit of being" and "I am not accustomed to being." We speak, with subtle differences, of the habits, customs, and practices of the Kikuyu. A man's habits, like his customs, may be usual or almost invariable, old or recent. A habit, like a practice, is something that we may fall into or get out of, that may become established or be abandoned, that we may be bound by or indulge in.

To explain a particular piece of behavior by saying "It's a habit" or "It's habitual" is to say that it is just one instance of what occurs regularly. To attribute it to "force of habit" is to suggest that the momentum gained by the regular performances of the past carried this performance through, even when it was pointless—e.g., checking the pulse of a man who is obviously dead.

It has commonly been suggested that to explain an action as "automatic" is the same as explaining it as done "from force of habit." The fact that the same action, e.g., stretching out your hand when the telephone rings, can be explained, even on the same occasion, in both these ways, is no doubt partly responsible for assimilating the two explanations.

That this is a mistake is clear from considering that an action can be automatic without its being done from force of habit, and done from force of habit without its being automatic. An action performed for the first and only time may be automatic, but not due to habit. If I am expecting you to telephone, and the phone rings, I may automatically conclude that it is you, although I do not conclude this from force of habit. An instinctive or reflex reaction, similarly, is automatic, but it is not due to force of habit. Contrariwise, I may from force of habit smoke three cigars a day, although I could not be said to smoke them automatically. "Partly," "almost," "semi-," "entirely," express degrees of being automatic; but something cannot be done with a degree of habit, even though it may be due to a partly formed habit.

To say that Y was on this occasion, or is usually, done "automatically" by a man or machine is to say that it was, or is, done after X without any intervening assistance. A machine that automatically refills itself when empty does not need any outside help between the two stages; a car with automatic transmission does not need a clutch and gear lever. Similarly, a man who automatically closes the door when he enters a room, or who automatically said "No" when asked for a loan, usually does, or on this occasion did, something as a consequence of something else, without any thinking occurring between the antecedent and the consequent.

Since an explanation of behavior as "automatic" is a reference to the lack of any intervening thought between the stimulus and the response, an automatic response is one that is made without thinking what one is doing. But there is no hint that what is done from force of habit need be done in any sense "without thinking." While it is certainly true that when something has become a habit, it can often be done without thinking about it, it is neither true that this is always so, nor is it true that it need ever be so.

I may straighten my tie from habit, and without thinking about it, but my habit of locking the doors at night is sometimes absent-mindedly and sometimes consciously manifested. Even though my rechecking of my mathematical calculations is due to an excellent habit that I acquired in my youth, it is never absent-minded, nor is it something I am able to do in my sleep. We have habits of which we are aware, and perhaps take pride in, and others of which we are quite unaware. When we speak of habit in connection with an inanimate object, naturally no question of attention or inattention arises. The reason why what we do automatically and what we do from force of habit so often coincide, and why, therefore, the two are confused, is that there is a strong natural connection between them. We try to establish the connection when inculcating automatic responses. To ensure that a type of performance Y is gone through whenever X happens, without one's having to think between them—that is, to ensure that Y is done automatically—one tries to form the habit of doing Y whenever X happens. Conversely, to ensure that doing Y whenever X happens becomes a habit involves training oneself to do Y whenever X happens, without having to think between them. But to have a habit of doing Y in circumstance X is not itself to do Y automatically in these circumstances. It is not a tautology to say that once you get into the habit of doing Y whenever X occurs, then you will be able to do Y automatically.

Traits. People are commonly described, in terms of their traits of character or intellect, as brave, conceited, timid, tactless, vivacious, conscientious, intelligent, stupid, pedantic, honest, considerate, etc. To describe them in these terms is to indicate the sorts of ways in which they frequently behave in certain sorts of circumstances. Unlike habitual behavior, the behavior in which traits are manifested is not invariable, inflexible, or stereotyped. It is not something that could characterize inanimate things nor, in some cases, even animals, but something that presupposes an intelligent agent, even in cases where the trait is stupidity or tactlessness. The sorts of things frequently done by a person described in any one of these ways are varied. Thus, a timid man hesitates to speak in company, retreats from dangers, lacks confidence, etc.; a conscientious man tries in various ways to cover every detail of what he conceives to be his duty.

Since to possess a trait is to have an inclination or proneness to do certain things in certain sorts of circumstances, to explain a piece of behavior as due to some trait is to classify it as an instance of this kind of behavior. When we say that someone hesitates to answer from timidity (because he is timid), or offers himself as a candidate for responsibilities beyond his competence from conceit (because he is conceited), or gives up his seat on the bus from considerateness (because he is considerate), we explain what he does by mentioning which of his characteristic inclinations, which of his traits, this piece of behavior manifests.

To have a proneness to do something is not to possess some psychological or physiological entity that could act as an antecedent cause of any behavior explained by it, in the same way as a light source is the cause of the light it manifests. No doubt, there are psychological and physiological antecedent causes that explain the acquisition and possession of our various traits; for example, my timidity and your conscientiousness may be due to our childhood training, and may have physiological bases in our brain structure. But the antecedent causes that explain the acquisition and possession of a proneness do not, except indirectly, explain the behavior that manifests that proneness on a particular occasion; the behavior is explained, not antecedently, but in a law-like manner, by the possession of that proneness of which it is a manifestation.

Nor will it do to suggest that these traits are feelings, which cause or trigger the behavior that they explain. For, first, people do not feel tactless or conscientious, vivacious or intelligent, pedantic or honest, conceited or considerate, even though part of the way in which they manifest these traits, aside from acting in certain ways, may sometimes consist in having certain feelings. For instance, the intelligent may feel confident before a problem, the conscientious worried in their work, and the pedantic pained when they see a rule broken. Secondly, even though people can at various times feel brave or stupid, frivolous or incompetent, the feeling is so far from being a necessary condition of their being any of these that it is in fact compatible with their lacking the trait in question. Further, we can be said correctly to possess the traits we do have, when they are not being exercised, even when we are asleep or too occupied to feel anything.

Inclination. I noted in the previous chapter that there are at least two logically distinct, although naturally related, senses in which we commonly speak of someone as being "inclined" to do something—namely, the sense in which being inclined is akin to a temptation, and the sense in which it is akin to a proneness. In the former sense, what we are inclined to do is a particular action; in the latter, a type of action. We can *feel* inclined in the former sense, but not in the latter. Hence, only what is animate can have the former sort of inclination. Further, a man may have pronenesses, but not temptations, of which he is unaware. We can refrain from doing what we feel tempted to do; what we are prone to do, however, is what we frequently do. We can feel inclined only to do, but we can be prone not only to do, but also to accomplish and to undergo. Feelings of inclination are measured by their strength, pronenesses by the number of their manifestations.

The two senses of "inclination" and "inclined to" are *logically* distinct; neither implies the other. A man who is inclined to split his infinitives may never have felt inclined to do so, indeed may even repudiate the imputation, while a man who often feels inclined to laugh at the mistakes of others may resolutely contain himself. In the case of a *unique* action, such as committing suicide, the man who feels inclined to do it cannot be sensibly described as prone to do it; contrariwise, in the case of a *result*, such as becoming puzzled, the man who frequently becomes so cannot feel like becoming so. When, however, the two senses of the phrases are applied to a single type of behavior, there is a strong natural connection between them. Normally, there is no reason why we should not do many of the things we feel tempted to do; conversely, what we are not prone to do may often be what we feel no inclination to do. It is not surprising, therefore, if, in practice, someone who is "inclined" in one sense is often also "inclined" in the other. This, together with the use of the one word, is no doubt why these two logically distinct senses have been assimilated.

In the feeling sense, "inclination" goes with such "general condition" feelings as indignation, fear, hope, or anxiety. To feel indignant is to feel inclined to protest; to feel afraid is to feel like running away. A sudden, momentary, or strong inclination—say, to kick someone downstairs —may relevantly be compared to an impulse or itching. When moral philosophers discuss motives in terms of "inclination" (e.g., Kant) or "desire" (e.g., Ross, Ewing, etc.), and when some contemporary psychologists equate motives with drives, tensions, wishes, desires, etc., what they may be offering is an explanation of conduct in terms of this kind of inclination.

"Inclination," in the frequency sense, goes with such traits as vanity, conceit, vivacity, tactlessness, and indolence. A vain man is inclined to boast, a tactless man to drop conversational bricks. People who are characterized by these inclinations need not feel anything; we do not feel vain, conceited, or vivacious, as we feel indignant or afraid. Talk of "impulse" and "itching" is out of place with such inclinations as traits of conceit and indolence.

We may legitimately explain a piece of human conduct by a frequency-inclination—e.g., a trait such as conceit or timidity—and also by a feeling-inclination—such as feeling indignant or feeling like bursting out laughing. A man may be said to have had a second swim because he felt inclined to do so or, quite differently, to have had a second helping of pudding because he is inclined to overestimate his capacity. But these two explanations employ quite different factors, and neither is like an explanation in terms of an end or purpose to be achieved. To interrupt a speaker because you have never acquired patience or courtesy, and to interrupt him because your indignation or fear makes you incapable of restraining yourself, are quite unlike each other; both again are unlike interrupting him in order to put him off his stride, or in order to create a diversion.

It is clear that an explanation in terms of a frequency-inclination, such as an explanation in terms of a habit or a trait, provides a reference to a law-like generalization about the agent's behavior; it explains the piece of behavior in question as an instance of a type. It is because Ryle (*The Concept of Mind*, 1949, ch. 4) explicitly took "motive" and "inclination" as synonyms that he gave the dispositional account of motives that, as I argued earlier, is a mistake. To remain silent because you are timid—that is, because you are prone to keep yourself back from possible risks—is not to act from a motive.

An explanation in terms of a feeling-inclination, on the other hand, makes no reference to a generalization or law. It is in one respect more like an explanation in terms of an antecedent cause, for it may mention some itch or impulse or urge that we feel prior to what we do and because of which we do it. Fear and indignation are typically what make us or drive us to do things. Yet, perhaps, a feeling-inclination, or even an impulse, is not an antecedent causal event, either. As the term suggests, what is "inclined to" something is already on the way to, or about to fall over into it, like a stone poised on the edge of a precipice, or a balloon expanding almost to bursting point. What is about to happen will happen, unless something prevents it or restrains it. Just as the poised stone will go over, or the balloon that is ready to burst will go off, unless they are stopped, so a man may be bursting with indignation or laughter and need to exercise restraint, or be restrained, so as not to do what he feels inclined to do. Fear, indignation, hope, anxiety, tenderness, pity, curiosity, interest, laughter, and joy are typically things we are full of, or even bursting with; they therefore typically contain a felt inclination to expand, or even to explode, into some form of behavior. Just as things that are on the brink of happening frequently happen, so people who feel inclined to do things frequently do them. But to explain the crash of the stone in terms of its poised position, the bursting of the balloon in terms of its state of expansion, or the occurrence of an event in terms of its having been about to happen, is not to point to an antecedent and separate event in the same way as the movement of one billiard ball is an event antecedent to and separate from the movement it causes in another billiard ball. Similarly, a felt inclination to do something does not explain the action by reference to an antecedent and separate happening, but by reference to the earlier state of the agent.

Mongrel-categorical explanations. We saw earlier that the relation between a specific concept, such as playing the piano or standing up, and a polymorphous concept, such as practicing for a concert or obeying an order, is such that the specific concept signifies something that may on a given occasion be the form that the thing signified by the polymorphous concept takes. Now some, but not all, polymorphous concepts are activity concepts—that is, they signify something that is actually going on. Of these polymorphous activity concepts, some, but not all, explain the specific activity. Thus, a man's playing of the piano may be explained by the fact that he is practicing for a concert, and his standing up may be explained by the fact that he is obeying an order. Such an explanatory statement Ryle has called a "mongrel-categorical" statement, because it both states that something unspecified is going on and also explains why it is going on. "He is practicing" is a mongrel-categorical statement relative to "He is playing the piano" and "He is obeying an order" is a mongrel-categorical statement relative to "He is standing up."

Sometimes such a statement takes a slightly different form. It now specifies what specific activity is going on, and, in a phrase that expresses the polymorphous concept, gives the reason for the specific activity. Thus, we may say "He is playing the piano for practice" or "He obediently stood up." It is clear that "for practice" and "obediently" do not give a causal antecedent of his action; they explain it as the specific form that the polymorphous activity took. On the other hand, they do not explain the action as a manifestation of an inclination, or a proneness, to do that type of action. There is no reason why the man who is playing the piano for practice should be prone to practice, nor why the man who obediently stands up should be generally obedient. "He stood up because he was obeying an order" does not give an explanation of the same kind as "He stood up because he is obedient." The specific actions that manifest a trait such as obedience or punctuality are, of course, obedient and punctual actions. But obedient and punctual actions—hence, their specific forms—are not necessarily the manifestations of traits of obedience and punctuality. One can perform an obedient or a punctual act quite uncharacteristically, and only once in one's life.

In other words, any action that is explainable by the trait of obedience or the trait of punctuality is necessarily an obedient or punctual act, but an action that is explainable as being an obedient or punctual act is not necessarily explainable as due to obedience or punctuality themselves. It is, therefore, a mistake to try to account for explanations that use words such as "obediently," "punctually," or "impatiently" in terms of inclinations to behave obediently, punctually or impatiently. The source of this mistake may be an ambiguity in such phrases as "from obedience," "from impatience," or "from vanity." It may be that to explain an action as having been done "from impatience or vanity" is to say either that it was done because the agent was behaving impatiently or vainly, or that it was done because the agent is impatient or vain. Behaving impatiently or vainly, however, is not the same thing as being impatient or vain.

Rule-governed behavior. The laws and generalizations I have mentioned so far are natural or descriptive laws— that is, statements of what actually happens or would happen under certain circumstances. There is no suggestion that what is in accordance with these laws literally follows, obeys, or is governed by them. These laws cannot be broken, although there may be exceptions to them—as, for instance, gases at low temperatures are exceptions to Boyle's Law. They may describe the way things happen or the way people behave. To explain something by reference to a descriptive law or a generalization of this sort is merely to point out that it is an example of what invariably or usually happens with that type of thing in these circumstances.

Sometimes, however, we explain what someone does by reference to a law or rule that he follows, consciously or unconsciously, as when what a man writes is explicable partly by rules of grammar, partly by canons of style, and partly by laws of logic. These may be called "prescriptive" laws. A man may do what he does because he is obeying certain rules, whether he realizes it or not, and whether he does so deliberately or as the result of practice. Wittgenstein once remarked that a stranger to this planet might be puzzled as to whether marching soldiers lifted their feet in a certain way because of a law of nature, like gravity, or because of some military rule.

It is obvious that explanations in terms of prescriptive laws cannot apply to things that do not obey rules, nor to what happens to us rather than what we do. The courses of stars and atoms cannot have this sort of explanation, nor can the triumphs and disasters that befall a man. Contrariwise, as I have argued in a previous section, and as Socrates insisted, the explanation for my handing over a present or obeying an order cannot consist solely of the descriptive laws of physiology; it must have a reference to the laws, customs, rules, etc., that people make, and either obey or disobey. Rational behavior is pre-eminently explicable in this way, because rational behavior is behavior that proceeds according to certain rules to which the agent subscribes.

TELEOLOGICAL EXPLANATIONS

One of the complaints that both Plato and Aristotle brought against their predecessors, the Milesian philosopher-scientists, was that they had neglected what has since come to be called the "teleological" type of explanation. This is an explanation that consists in mentioning the end (*telos*), or purpose, that for the sake of which something is done, or that toward which it is a means. We might explain the taking of exercise by noting that it is done for the sake of one's health, or in order to be healthy; we could say that a candidate took the examination a second time in order to improve his mark.

The notions of *end, purpose*, and *means* imply an agent, someone who does something for the sake of something else, whose efforts are directed toward the end, who adopts means and methods, and follows certain rules and principles. Teleological explanations have commonly been resorted to by theologians, who have tended to explain everything as part of the purposes of the divine mind. Philosophers and scientists, such as Descartes and Leibniz, who wanted to save the human mind from the mechanistic causality of the rising sciences of the sixteenth and seventeenth centuries, explained the workings of the mind in terms of a "final" cause. Philosophers who supposed that all explanations are causal naturally felt that an explanation in terms of an end also had to be translated into one in terms of an antecedent cause. An apparently obvious way to achieve this offered itself. For, as early as Aristotle, it was assumed, first, that to say that a certain end or purpose explains an action is the same as saying that the agent's desire for that end or his purpose explains the action; secondly, that to say that the desire for X explains the doing of X is to say that desire here is an antecedent cause. Freud thought of his explanatory terms "conscious motives" and "unconscious motives" as names of entities, whether desires or ideas, stored in the conscious or unconscious parts of the mind, and working like the mechanical and dynamic forces of physics. Many psychologists and physiologists who have explained purposive behavior as due to "drives," and the hedonistic philosophers and psychologists who alleged that all is done for pleasure, have often treated "drives" and "pleasure" as antecedent mental or physiological springs of action.

To reject this reduction of teleological explanation to that of an antecedent causal kind is not to deny that a person's desires and beliefs are relevant to his ends and purposes, and that the former must be taken into account in an analysis of the latter. It is only to deny, as I have already done, that an explanation in terms of desire is an explanation in terms of an antecedent cause.

Motives. I have argued in a previous section that *motive* signifies a type of explanation, rather than any kind of factor that appears in an explanation. Hence, neither feelings, thoughts, dispositions, intentions, nor even desires, necessarily provide explanations of the motive type. To say that I shook from fear, that I blushed at the thought of what I had done, that I hesitated from timidity, that I was loitering with intent to steal, or that I took something because I wanted it, is not to provide the motive for what I did.

To provide the motive for a deed is to note that desire for the sake of satisfying which the deed was done—assuming that what was done was not itself what was desired, but a deed that the agent thought would bring about or would amount to what was desired. Motives do not apply in situations in which something is done for its own sake, but only where it is done for the sake of something else. Because what the agent did was something that he thought would have such and such an effect, or would amount to so and so, what he did must have been intentional. It could not have been merely a reflex reaction or a habit, nor an accident, nor something done without his realizing it.

Sometimes, in suggesting a motive we refer to a specific desire, as when a man's desire to prevent his uncle from changing his will is cited as his motive for murder. At other times we refer to the object that he desired to obtain, as when a man's motive is said to be money or power. Frequently we refer to one of those traits the possession of which indicates that the agent's life is properly characterized by a desire for so and so, or one of those emotions that involve the desire for such and such. Since greedy men want possessions, ambitious men want power, and vindictive men want to get even with their enemies, traits such as greediness, ambition, or vindictiveness can be cited as motives for action. Because revenge involves wanting to hurt someone for a supposed injury, and jealousy involves wanting to remove rivals, emotions such as revenge and jealousy can also provide motives.

Motive-explanations refer to that further thing for the sake of which something is done; they are therefore teleological. Since the factor they contain is a desire for something, our previous argument that desires are not causal antecedents is also proof that motives cannot be regarded as kinds of causes.

Purposes. An obvious example of teleological explanation is that in terms of purpose. Indeed, "purposive" and "teleological" have sometimes been equated. But we must distinguish between "purpose" as it is used of happenings and as it is used of actions. An instrument, such as a carburetor or the human heart, has a purpose—that is, a function; but only intelligent beings, whether animal or human, can do things on purpose or for a purpose.

To do X purposely or on purpose is not the same thing as doing X for a purpose. Since one cannot do X for the purpose of doing X—as one can do X with the intention of doing X—but only for the purpose of doing or achieving Y, to do X on purpose implies doing X for a (further) purpose. Now, to characterize some deed as done for a particular purpose is to suggest a reason for doing it; hence, we speak of someone's "reason or purpose" and of "the point or purpose" of something. It may have been done for the sole or express purpose, for a special, a practical, a selfish, or an unlawful purpose, for a variety of purposes, or for no obvious purpose at all. Various things may serve, be needed for, lend themselves to, depend on, affect, or be appropriate to, my purposes or yours or the law's. Someone's purpose may be to perform a certain task or to achieve a certain result, to do so and so, or to become or to get such and such. To do anything for a purpose is to do it in order to do or achieve something else. The purpose is that for which it is done.

Motives and purposes are related, in that to refer to the motive is to indicate the desire for the sake of which something is done, while to refer to the purpose is to indicate that for which there is this desire. Thus, if I murder someone in order to get his money, my motive is a desire for money, my purpose is to get the money. But, of course, motives are not the same as purposes. Things are done for a purpose, but from a motive. Purposes, unlike motives, can be served, achieved, or accomplished.

Intentions. Philosophers have often and recently argued that intentions provide explanations for behavior. This is a mistake, I think, partly resulting from the assimilation of intentions with either motives or purposes, and partly due to the fact that what is done from a motive or for a purpose is necessarily done intentionally, and, indeed, with an intention. Since I have in an earlier section tried to show the differences between motives and intentions, I shall here confine myself to the notions of *purpose* and *intention*.

First, intentions and purposes are different. Purposes, like aims, may be unachieved or fail to be accomplished; they may be served or unaffected by things. Intentions, like plans, are sometimes unfulfilled or they fail to be carried out. Intentions relate to actions; purposes, to ends. Purposes imply intentions, but intentions do not necessarily imply purposes. If I purposely drop a catch, I do this intentionally; but if I glance idly around the room, I glance around intentionally, but not purposely. If I have to phone A, B and C, and am not concerned about the order in which I do it, then, if I phone A before B, I do this intentionally, but not necessarily purposely; whereas, if what I have to say to B depends on what A tells me, I will purposely, and of course intentionally, phone A before B. My purpose in doing something is my reason for doing it, in the sense of what I am trying to do, or what I want to accomplish by doing it. My intention in doing it is what

I have in mind in doing it. If I have a purpose, I may have that in mind; but what I have in mind in doing something need not be a purpose, for there may be no purpose. It is significant that I do things *with* an intention, but *for* a purpose.

Secondly, to specify an intention, unlike specifying a purpose, is not necessarily to give an explanation. We do not naturally speak of "the reason or intention" and "the point or intention" in the same way as we speak of "the reason or purpose" and "the point or purpose" of an action. Nothing serves or lends itself to our intention as it does to our purpose; things are not judged as useful for our intention as they are for our purpose. To say that we did something purposely is to suggest that we had a reason for doing it, but we need have no reason for what we do intentionally. Similarly, the (further) purpose for which we do something is necessarily a reason for doing it; but the (further) intention with which we do it is not necessarily a reason. Thus, to say that I am going to Australia with the intention of staying not more than a year is not to give any explanation of my going to Australia. What has misled philosophers here, I think, is partly that the same thing may be cited, even on the same occasion, both as my intention and as my purpose in doing something. Thus, I may go to Australia with the intention of and for the purpose of visiting my grandchildren. Since my purpose— namely, to visit my grandchildren—explains my going to Australia, it is easy to suppose that my intention, which also is to visit my grandchildren, therefore also provides a reason, indeed the same reason, for my journey. But that purpose and intention are not the same is clear from the fact that, while another intention with which I go to Australia might be to return after a year, that cannot be another purpose for which I go there.

For Further Reading

Chapter 1.

On the nature of philosophical argument:

Passmore, J., *Philosophical Reasoning*, London: Duckworth, 1961, ch. 7.

Ryle, G., *Philosophical Arguments*, Oxford: Clarendon Press, 1945.

Waismann, F., "How I see philosophy" in *Contemporary British Philosophy*, Series III (ed. H. D. Lewis), London: Allen and Unwin, 1956, esp. pp. 471–82.

Wittgenstein, L., *Philosophical Investigations*, Oxford: Blackwell, 1953, sects. 118–33.

On the nature of concepts:

Bruner, J. S., Goodnow, J. J. and Austin, G. A., *A Study of Thinking*, New York: Wiley, 1956, chs. 1 and 2.

Geach, P. T., *Mental Acts*, London: Routledge and Kegan Paul, 1958, sects. 5–11.

Price, H. H., *Thinking and Experience*, London: Hutchinson, 1953, ch. 11.

Thomson, R., *The Psychology of Thinking*, Harmondsworth, Eng.: Penguin Books, 1959, chs. 4 and 5.

On the place of language in philosophy:

Austin, J. L., "A Plea for Excuses" in *Proceedings of the Aristotelian Society*, LVII (1957), 1–30.

Ryle, G., "Ordinary Language" in *The Philosophical Review*, LXII (1953), 167–86.

Chapter 2.

For a general history of theories of mind:

Peters, R. S. (ed.), *Brett's History of Psychology*, London: Allen and Unwin, 1953.

For extracts from Plato to the present:

Dennis, W., *Readings in the History of Psychology*, New York: Appleton-Century-Crofts, 1948.

Rand, B., *The Classical Psychologists*, Boston: Houghton
    Mifflin, 1912.
Reeves, J. W., *Body and Mind in Western Thought*,
    Harmondsworth, Eng.: Penguin Books, 1958, Part
    Two.

On the Political Theory:

Crombie, I. M., *An Examination of Plato's Doctrines*, Lon-
    don: Routledge and Kegan Paul, 1963, vol. I, ch. 7,
    sect. 5.
Mayo, B., *Ethics and the Moral life*, London: Macmillan,
    1958, pp. 125–46.
Plato, *Republic*, pp. 434–44; *Phaedo*, pp. 70c–76e.
Ryle, G., *Dilemmas*, Cambridge: Cambridge University
    Press, 1954, pp. 63–66.

On the Physical Theory:

The extracts from seventeenth, eighteenth and nineteenth
century writers in Dennis, Rand and Reeves.

Ryle, G., *The Concept of Mind*, London: Hutchinson,
    1949, ch. 1.
Sluckin, W., *Minds and Machines*, Harmondsworth, Eng.:
    Penguin Books, 1954, ch. 10.

On the Freudian Theory:

Freud's theoretical works. A bibliography of these appears
in the *Standard Edition*, edited by J. Strachey, London: Ho-
garth Press, 1953– , vol. 14, pp. 259–60. The most relevant
here are:

The Ego and the Id (1923), Standard Edition, vol. 19.
"The Unconscious" (1915), Standard Edition, vol. 14.
New Introductory Lectures on Psycho-analysis (1933),
    Standard Edition, vol. 22, ch. 31.
An Outline of Psycho-analysis (1940), Standard Edition,
    vol. 23.

Ellis, A., "An operational reformulation of some of the
    basic principles of psycho-analysis" in *Minnesota Studies
    in the Philosophy of Science* (eds. H. Feigl and M.
    Scriven), Minneapolis: Minnesota University Press, 1956,
    vol. I, pp. 131–54.
MacIntyre, A. C., *The Unconscious*, London: Routledge
    and Kegan Paul, 1958, chs. 2 and 3.

Skinner, B. F., "Critique of Psycho-analytic Concepts and Theories" in *Minnesota Studies in the Philosophy of Science* (eds. H. Feigl and M. Scriven), Minneapolis: Minnesota University Press, 1956, vol. I, pp. 77–87.

On the Functional Theory:

(a) Aristotle, *De Anima,* esp. pp. 402a–15b; *Nicomachean Ethics,* pp. 1098a, 1102a and 1102b.

(b) Angell, J. R., "The Province of Functional Psychology" in *Psychological Review,* XIV (1907), 61–91, reprinted in Dennis, *op. cit.*

Broadbent, D. E., *Behaviour,* London: Eyre and Spottiswoode, 1961, ch. 1.

McDougall, W., *Psychology: The Study of Behaviour,* London: Williams and Norgate, 1912, chs. 1 and 3.

———, *An Outline of Psychology,* London: Methuen, 1923, ch. 1.

Titchener, E. B., "The Postulates of a Structural Psychology" in *The Philosophical Review,* VII (1898), 449–65, reprinted in Dennis, *op. cit.*

Tolman, E. C., *Purposive Behavior in Animals and Men,* New York: Century, 1932, chs. 1 and 25.

Watson, J. B., "Psychology as the Behaviorist views it," in *Psychological Review,* XX (1913), 158–77, reprinted in Dennis, *op. cit.*

Chapter 3.

On attention-concepts in general:

Austin, J. L., "A Plea for Excuses" in *Proceedings of the Aristotelian Society,* LVII (1957), 1–30.

Place, U. T., "The Concept of Heed" in *British Journal of Psychology,* XLV (1954), 243–55.

Ryle, G., *The Concept of Mind,* London: Hutchinson, 1949, pp. 135–49.

White, A. R., *Attention,* Oxford: Blackwell, 1964.

For discussion of specific attention-concepts, consult the above together with:

On interest:

Arnold, F., "The Psychology of Interest" in *Psychological Review,* XII (1906), 221–38, 291–315.

Berlyne, D. E., "'Interest' as a psychological concept" in *British Journal of Psychology*, XXXIX (1949), 184–95.

On enjoyment:

Peters, R. S., *The Concept of Motivation*, London: Routledge and Kegan Paul, 1958, ch. 5.

Ryle, G., "Pleasure" in *Proceedings of the Aristotelian Society*, Suppl. XXVIII (1954), 135–46.

For the ideas of "polymorphous" and "mongrel-categorical":

Ryle, G., *The Concept of Mind*, London: Hutchinson, 1949, 135–49.

————, "Thinking and Language" in *Proceedings of the Aristotelian Society*, Suppl. XXV (1951), 67–69.

Chapter 4.

The philosophy of thought:

Price, H. H., *Thinking and Experience*, London: Hutchinson, 1953, esp. chs. 4, 8, 10.

Ryle, G., *The Concept of Mind*, London: Hutchinson, 1949, ch. 9.

————, "Thinking and Language" in *Proceedings of the Aristotelian Society*, Suppl. XXV (1951), 65–82.

Wittgenstein, L., *Philosophical Investigations*, Oxford: Blackwell, 1953, pt. I, sects. 316–61, and pt. II, pp. 214–23.

The psychology of thought:

Humphrey, G., *Thinking: An Introduction to its Experimental Psychology*, London: Methuen, 1951.

Leeper, R., "Cognitive Processes" in *Handbook of Experimental Psychology* (ed. S. S. Stevens), New York: Wiley, 1951, ch. 19.

Thomson, R., *The Psychology of Thinking*, Harmondsworth, Eng.: Penguin Books, 1959.

Chapter 5.

Armstrong, D. M., *Bodily Sensations*, London: Routledge and Kegan Paul, 1962.

Bedford, E., "Emotions" in *Proceedings of the Aristotelian Society*, LVII (1957), 281–304.

Kenny, A., *Action, Emotion and Will*, London: Routledge and Kegan Paul, 1963, chs. 1–3.

Peters, R. S. and Mace, C. A., "Emotions and the Category of Passivity" in *Proceedings of the Aristotelian Society*, LXII (1962), 117–42.

Pitcher, G., "Emotion" in *Mind*, LXXIV (1965), 326–46.

Ryle, G., *The Concept of Mind*, London: Hutchinson, 1949, ch. 4.

———, "Feelings" in *The Philosophical Quarterly*, I (1951), 193–205.

Wittgenstein, L., *Philosophical Investigations*, Oxford: Blackwell, 1953, sects. 244–315, 404–11.

On the psychology of emotion:

Gardiner, H. N., Metcalfe, R. C. and Beebe-Center, J. G., *Feeling and Emotion: A History of Theories*, New York: American Book Co., 1937.

Krech, D. and Crutchfield, R. S., *Elements of Psychology*, New York: Knopf, 1958, chs. 9 and 12.

Woodworth, R. S. and Schlosberg, H., *Experimental Psychology*, London: Methuen, 1961, chs. 5–7.

Chapter 6.

Anscombe, G. E. M., *Intention*, Oxford: Blackwell, 1957.

Kenny, A., *Action, Emotion and Will*, London: Routledge and Kegan Paul, 1963, ch. 4.

Melden, A. I., *Free Action*, London: Routledge and Kegan Paul, 1961.

Ryle, G., *The Concept of Mind*, London: Hutchinson, 1949, chs. 4 and 5, sect. 4.

Sutherland, N. S., "Motives as Explanations" in *Mind*, LXVIII (1959), 145–59.

On explanation in psychology:

Peters, R. S., *The Concept of Motivation*, London: Routledge and Kegan Paul, 1958.

Smith, F. V., *Explanations of Human Behaviour*, London: Constable, 1951.

Taylor, C., *The Explanation of Behaviour*, London: Routledge and Kegan Paul, 1964.

Index